American Association of Community Colleges

National Profile

of Community Colleges:

Trends & Statistics

KENT A. PHILLIPPE AND LEILA GONZÁLEZ SULLIVAN

4th Edition

The American Association of Community Colleges (AACC) is the primary advocacy organization for the nation's community colleges. The association represents more than 1,100 two-year, associate degree–granting institutions and more than 11 million students. AACC promotes community colleges through six strategic action areas: national and international recognition and advocacy, learning and accountability, leadership development, economic and workforce development, connectedness across AACC membership, and international and intercultural education. Information about AACC and community colleges may be found at www.aacc.nche.edu.

Editor: Deanna D'Errico
Design: Brian Gallagher
Printer: Kirby Lithographic

Community College Press
American Association of Community Colleges
One Dupont Circle, NW
Suite 410
Washington, DC 20036

Printed in the United States of America.

ISBN 0-87117-365-4

CONTENTS

LIST OF FIGURES AND TABLES

CHAPTER III

CHAPTER V

PREFACE

The fourth edition of the *National Profile of Community Colleges: Trends and Statistics* provides a broad overview of America's community colleges as they enter their second century. Introductory text for each chapter gives the reader context, complemented by charts and graphs to provide a more detailed representation of enrollment, funding, and other key issues.

Chapter 1 recounts the history of community colleges and summarizes some of the more pressing issues facing them today. Chapter 2 provides detailed information and demographics concerning enrollment at community colleges and puts it in perspective with the rest of higher education. Chapter 3 describes the impact of community colleges on students and their communities through measures such as degree and certificate completion, employment data, and educational attainment within the general population. Chapter 4 offers a view of staffing at community colleges, from the presidency and senior administration to faculty and support staff. Chapter 5 focuses on the financial aspects of community colleges, as they affect the institution and its students. Chapter 6 presages trends and issues that will define the community college of the future.

In the 21st century, community colleges must continue to be flexible and innovative to meet the varied, complex, and changing needs of students and communities.

Increased national visibility and urgent demands such as our post–September 11, 2001, economy require new and inventive responses. As enrollments rise and demands for accountability grow, the colleges must balance the challenge of ensuring both access—the open door to historically underserved populations—and success—measurable attainment in the form of degrees, certifications, and other benchmarks of achievement. The *National Profile* helps document these trends.

The *National Profile's* data come from several sources, including surveys conducted by the American Association of Community Colleges (AACC), scholars from the community college field, the U.S. Department of Education, the U.S. Census Bureau, and the Bureau of Labor Statistics. Because of differing methodologies, numbers may vary across the many tables and figures despite efforts to report statistics consistently. The most recent data available were used to create these tables. Many data sets are not immediately available after collection, as they must go through internal review processes at the organization that collects them.

Overall enrollment is reported using full-year unduplicated headcounts. This method counts each student once for the academic year regardless of the number of terms in which he or she attended classes. Breakdowns within student enrollments are not available for full-year, unduplicated headcounts. Therefore, race, sex, age, and other

demographic information are reported based on fall term attendance, which accounts for 60% of the full-year enrollment. In some cases, statistics may not add up to 100% because of rounding.

The *National Profile* focuses on credit enrollment at community colleges because no accurate national data exist about noncredit activity at community colleges. The U.S. Department of Education provides definitions and a collection mechanism for credit enrollment through the Integrated Postsecondary Education Data System (IPEDS), but noncredit enrollment has no equivalent.

Based on contacts with states that collect some of this information, AACC estimates that more than 5 million students each year participate in some form of noncredit educational activities at community colleges. Noncredit coursework is a substantial and growing component of community college activity—far more than personal interest or recreational classes. Career, technical, and vocational studies are important components, with many noncredit classes leading to some form of vendor certification. Most colleges also offer noncredit, contracted training customized to fit the needs of local business and industry, government agencies, and other organizations. AACC hopes to see an increase in the reporting of noncredit enrollment and will continue to monitor the data as they are available.

This book would not have been possible without the hard work and support of many people. Sara McPhee, Arina Lindley, and Cynthia Vervena provided assistance in collecting and summarizing the data presented in many of the tables. Deanna D'Errico provided significant support in editing and guiding this publication through to completion.

Margaret Rivera provided support throughout the production of this publication, reviewing manuscripts and data and providing general oversight to this project. ⊕

I
Community Colleges Past and Present

The seeds of the American community college were planted just before the Civil War when Congress passed the Morrill Act in 1862. This legislation was the first concrete expression of the belief that all citizens, not just a privileged few, should have access to higher education. Extended to the former Confederate states in 1890, the Morrill Act granted each state 30,000 acres of federal land per member of its congressional delegation to establish a university, hence the term *land grant*. These public universities were to prepare students for careers in agriculture, engineering, and military science: In effect, the new public institutions constituted the first national workforce development initiatives. At the same time, the concept of basic education for all Americans was expanding with the rise of public high schools that extended schooling beyond the elementary grades.

At the turn of the century, yet another innovation was introduced in American education when it became apparent that some means was needed to bridge the span between high schools and universities. Students who sought a traditional liberal arts education could apply for admission to public and private colleges and universities, according to Cohen and Brawer (2003). However, these traditional institutions generally did not address the need for trained workers to serve the industries that were emerging in the first decades of the 20th century, nor were sufficient seats available for all who sought entry to higher education. The pressure to train workers, coupled with the growing importance of science and technology, gave impetus to the move to establish two-year colleges that combined liberal education with college-level vocational instruction. Called junior colleges, these original institutions were usually branches of either local school districts or universities.

Joliet Junior College, established in 1901, is the oldest continuously operating public two-year college in the United States. Grounded in the ideas of educators William Rainey Harper, president of the University of Chicago, and J. Stanley Brown, principal of the public high school in Joliet, Illinois, the new institution offered a fifth and sixth year of study beyond high school that was comparable to the first two years of college. High school graduates who lacked money to attend or were not accepted at the highly competitive universities of the era now had access to postsecondary education. Even before 1901, a number of two-year private colleges existed around the country, in part to train teachers for the growing public education system.

The new model gained popularity rapidly, and by 1910, 5% of American 18-year-olds were enrolling in colleges and universities, including the newly created junior colleges. During that same period, California legislators provided their high schools with funding to offer the first two years of college study, and by 1921 that state had established 21 colleges, the largest system of public two-year colleges in the country. Missouri,

Minnesota, and other states followed suit. In the 1930s there were more than 200 public and 300 private two-year colleges across the nation, offering job training and other education programs that became lifelines for people who were unemployed during the Great Depression.

The year 1921 marked another significant moment in the life of American community colleges with the establishment of the American Association of Junior Colleges. The organization was later renamed the American Association of Community and Junior Colleges. In 1992 the name was changed again to the American Association of Community Colleges (AACC), with the understanding that junior, technical, private, and proprietary two-year institutions could all fit within the term *community college*. This national organization was conceived originally as a place for two-year college presidents to exchange ideas, formulate policy, and build their own leadership skills. Today, the organization has grown to embrace all those who work or study at community colleges and has become the national voice for community colleges, providing advocacy, leadership, and service for its member institutions.

Post–World War II community colleges broadened the array of vocational programs they offered in order to accommodate returning soldiers

who used the GI Bill to prepare for jobs and ease their reentry into a peacetime economy. Spurred by the endorsement of the Truman Commission in 1947, the colleges became more than ever a primary point of entry into higher education in the United States. The Truman Commission called for public post-secondary education for all Americans and recommended that a national network of community colleges be established to provide universal access.

The 1960s were truly boom years for the community college movement. About 45% of all 18-year-olds, the so-called baby boomers who were the children of the returning WWII soldiers, enrolled in college. This was the era when many parents concluded that college was a necessity rather than a luxury for their children. It was also a time of great disagreement over the Vietnam War, and many took advantage of draft deferments for full-time students, causing enrollments to soar. More than one million students attended the more than 700 two-year colleges that had sprung up around the country as local leaders realized the value of such institutions to their communities. During that decade, more than 450 new colleges opened their doors, and a major facilities construction boom occurred as a result of the strong economy (see Cohen & Brawer, 2003).

The concept of the comprehensive community college was defined and refined in the 1960s as local sponsors called on the colleges to provide a broad range of programs: transfer education, vocational training, noncredit courses, customized training for business and industry, cultural enrichment opportunities, and a host of other services. Three types of degrees were offered—associate in arts, associate in sciences, and associate in applied sciences—with the first two focused on preparation for transfer to four-year colleges and universities and the last focused on preparation for entry-level employment. Many certificate programs were designed as well to address highly specific training needs. Although not all institutions offered all of these options, the majority did so.

The 1960s were significant for another development: the founding of tribal colleges. These institutions serve a dual purpose, providing access to postsecondary education for Native Americans while also preserving traditional tribal cultures. The 31 colleges in operation today are relatively small, receiving funds primarily from the Bureau of Indian Affairs. Their greatest assets are dedicated faculty and staff, mainly composed of Native Americans, and finding sufficient resources to serve their students is a continuous struggle. A few offer bachelor's degrees, but most tribal colleges offer the associate degree as their highest credential.

The independent, nonprofit, two-year colleges faced many challenges during the last half of the 20th century. At one time more numerous than their sister public institutions, the independent colleges saw the balance shift in the mid 1950s when they became less able to compete with the lower costs and greater resources of the public sector. Some ceased operations and others merged with universities or became baccalaureate-granting institutions. Today there are fewer than 150 independent two-year colleges in operation, many of them single-sex or religiously affiliated.

Now, 100 years after the first visionary leaders made the American dream of universal access to higher education a reality through a nation-wide network of two-year colleges, these institutions play a central role in the lives of millions of people and their communities. In Fall 2002, 11.6 million students were enrolled in the 1,158 public, independent, and tribal community colleges, including 6.6 million students taking courses for credit and 5 million taking noncredit courses, most of whom were partici-pating in short-term job training. Most Americans have a community college, branch campus, or extension center within an hour's drive of their homes, and they turn to their local college whenever they have learning needs over the course of a lifetime. For many communities, these colleges are also the center of recreational and cultural life in the area. Furthermore, community colleges have been recog-nized as a critical element of the eco-nomic well-being of the nation, and countries around the world are look-ing to adapt this model for their own postsecondary education systems.

Contemporary community col-leges face numerous challenges as they enter their second century of service. American higher education is evolving from a European model introduced in the Middle Ages to a form that is not yet fully defined. Clearly, any new model must be marked by greater flexibility, fewer boundaries, and more varied struc-tures. The hallmark of community colleges has always been flexible and rapid response to learners' needs, so they are well positioned to lead this evolution. In the meantime and for the near future, the colleges must address these significant challenges:

- limited funding in combination with substantial enrollment growth
- increasing demand for accounta-bility
- growing diversity in the student body
- renewed emphasis on workforce and teacher preparation
- constantly changing technologies
- impending turnover in community college leadership

The paramount challenge, of course, is how to fund a broad range of services for a growing student body when resources continue to be limit-ed. The early years of the current decade have been difficult ones for community colleges as state funding for higher education has been reduced drastically because of the depressed economy. Colleges' alloca-tions have been significantly reduced, particularly in those states that collect the greater portion of revenues through income and sales taxes—which are the revenue sources most likely to be affected by an economic downturn. In fact, state tax funding for higher education in 2000 (based on per capita personal income) was $23.4 billion below the peak expen-diture reached in 1979, according to Mortenson (2000) of The Pell Institute for the Study of Opportunity in Higher Education.

Community colleges have used some traditional and some new strategies for coping with their reduced financial resources. Many have cut faculty and staff positions or delayed filling vacancies. Equipment purchases, facilities maintenance, and construction projects have also been postponed. In an effort to bring in additional revenues, tuition and fees at the colleges increased an average of 12% in 2002.

On the more creative side, some colleges have forged new partnerships with private industry and nonprofit organizations to support costly career program curricula such as nursing, automotive technology, and information technology. Others have worked with their states to introduce slot machines or other means of increasing revenues for education. In New Jersey, the governor and the community colleges signed a formal agreement, the New Jersey Compact, which makes these institutions the preferred providers of workforce training, working in conjunction with the U.S. Departments of Commerce, Labor, and Education. The New Jersey colleges will also partner with the AFL-CIO to offer apprentice training. Still other colleges are taking advantage of new federal funds for special programs such as homeland security.

The funding stresses of the early 2000s must be placed in the context of the growing demand for postsecondary education. Between 1998 and 2002, enrollments in two-year colleges increased by 18%, while four-year institutions grew at a rate of only 10% (National Center for Education Statistics [NCES], 2004e). There are many reasons for this enrollment increase, including a larger college-age population (the baby boom echo),

the need to retrain workers displaced by a poor economy, and the greater numbers of people of color undertaking college studies. The rising cost of attending four-year colleges and universities has also pushed many students to begin their studies at a community college, where tuition is substantially lower and they can save on the overall cost of a college education. Nevertheless, one consequence of the funding difficulties community colleges have experienced in recent years is that they have been forced to turn away hundreds of thousands of students because they simply do not have the resources to serve them.

There are signs that this grim economic picture is changing. In 2004, a number of states—including California, Virginia, North Carolina, and Arizona—increased their allocations for community colleges after several years of budget cuts. These increased funds are certainly welcome, but it will take the colleges several years to catch up and restore services they reduced or eliminated during the lean years. And, given the trend toward continued enrollment growth, the colleges will need to manage well the resources they do have in order to continue offering the highest quality and greatest range of education services for their communities.

Another challenge for the present

and the immediate future is the continuing demand for accountability. The reduction in government support for higher education has not lessened the interest in holding colleges accountable; rather, it has produced an even greater desire to ensure that public dollars are spent wisely and that there is a real return on investment. The Education Commission of the States (2000) reported that as of 2001, 19 states had some form of performance funding tying a percentage of budget allocations to an institution's achievement on specified performance criteria. Twenty-seven states had performance budgeting requirements that allow governors and legislators to consider campus achievement on key indicators as one factor in determining allocations. Thirty-nine states had performance reporting programs mandating that colleges provide periodic updates regarding their performance on key indicators, but they were not tied to funding. Many states combine either performance funding or performance budgeting with reporting requirements.

Working with state agencies and education organizations, community colleges have become actively engaged in identifying key indicators that give a true picture of their effectiveness. This is a very complex process in light of the diverse education goals students have when enrolling and the broad mission of the colleges, ranging from transfer education to career preparation to community development and enrichment. States now specify between 3 and 37 key indicators of institutional effectiveness, such as graduation rates, transfer rates, passing scores on licensure exams, student satisfaction, and job placement data. To address these accountability mandates, community colleges have developed much more sophisticated means of collecting and analyzing data, and many have increased their research staffs.

The growing diversity of the student body is another challenge that is expected to continue over the next 20 to 30 years, based on population projections. One group of students includes recent high school graduates who plan to transfer to baccalaureate-granting institutions. Another group is somewhat older, often lacks basic skills and English language skills, and seeks job skills for immediate entry into the workforce. Yet another group is composed of workers who want to diversify or upgrade job skills through either credit or noncredit study. Finally, there is a group that seeks enrichment through coursework and recreational or cultural activities. Of course, these groups include both men and women and people of all colors, abilities, academic preparation, and ages. Community colleges must address the lifelong learning demands of all these groups through a comprehensive array of services that is constantly being adjusted. This requires greater capacity overall and the willingness to let go of services that are no longer useful while rapidly deploying new services targeted to specific, even individualized, needs. Ultimately, this challenge focuses on ensuring students' educational success over a lifetime regardless of their backgrounds and goals.

The contemporary community college is also challenged by the need to maintain the currency of curricula in light of workforce preparation mandates, competition from other education providers, and the globalized economy. New programs appear almost daily as colleges develop programs that prepare workers for emerging career fields, such as information technology security and homeland security.

To meet workforce preparation mandates while addressing the current shortage of teachers, many colleges have been prompted to strengthen existing teacher training programs or add new ones. They have established more formal articulation agreements with baccalaureate teacher preparation programs so that students can move smoothly from one institution to another and reduce time in training. In some cases, these agreements involve dual enrollment and special support services. Still other two-year colleges have introduced baccalaureate teacher training programs of their own. For example, in 2003, a new College of Education at Miami Dade College (FL) began offering bachelor's degree programs leading to teacher certification in exceptional student education (K–12), secondary mathematics (6–12), and secondary science (6–12) with concentrations in biology, chemistry, earth science, and physics.

The decision to offer bachelor's degrees at community colleges is the subject of considerable discussion at the moment. On one hand, proponents state that this level of programming is needed to serve students who would have difficulty engaging in study at distant universities. If access to higher education is the issue, then these degrees make sense. The proximity and lower costs of programs at community colleges are positive factors in the eyes of these supporters. On the other hand, opponents insist that offering bachelor's degrees is a form of "mission creep" that distracts from the community college's true purpose and may divert needed resources away from associate-level programs. Opponents also feel that having both levels of degrees on the same campus could create a kind of classism among faculty and students.

Coping with continuously changing technologies is yet another challenge for community colleges.

Maintaining current, up-to-date laboratories, training facilities, and curricula for students is critical to ensure that exiting students take with them skills that not only meet market demands but also will make them competitive in the current marketplace. Now and for the foreseeable future, every instructional and administrative process will be affected by technology. At present, the majority of faculty have introduced some form of technology into their teaching repertoire, ranging from simple PowerPoint presentations in the classroom to full-scale online courses and degree programs. Computerized simulations, streaming video, synchronous and asynchronous discussions, and many other technology-assisted instructional activities are becoming the norm. E-mail is the standard for communication between instructors and students, and course management systems such as WebCT and Blackboard are widely used. As a natural consequence of these instructional innovations, colleges are under considerable pressure to provide state-of-the-art equipment, the latest software, and regular training for faculty.

On the administrative side, after an initial sluggish period, colleges are truly becoming paperless—replacing catalogs, personnel and procedures manuals, budget materials, student records, and many other materials with online versions. Moreover, colleges are finding that such changes involve more than simple transitions from paper to electronic formats; each process must be reconceived and redesigned, with the incentive of reducing processing time and allowing greater access to useful data for faculty and staff. Technologies are also affecting facilities. New construction generally takes the form of "smart buildings," where many functions are controlled by computer, and older facilities are being retrofitted to be smart as well.

The high cost of all of these new technology tools, together with the related staff training and technical support costs, places great pressure on colleges to acquire sufficient fiscal resources and manage these wisely. This is particularly difficult during years when the American economic cycle is in a downturn, which happens at some point in each decade. During these periods, college leaders must try to keep education costs affordable while also ensuring that enough dollars flow into the institution from public and private sources to support all operations, including those that are technology based.

The many challenges facing community colleges today must be addressed at the same time that a significant turnover in leadership is occurring. A survey conducted in 2001 by AACC (Shults, 2001) showed that between one quarter and one half of presidents and senior administrators expected to retire in the next three to five years. Similar rates have been projected for senior faculty and support staff. The retirement exodus in this decade will entail a significant loss of institutional knowledge, but it will also present opportunities to do things differently and bring rising stars among administrators and faculty to the fore. Fortunately, community colleges have a long history of resilience and innovation that will allow them to make the leadership transition and find effective solutions for contemporary and future challenges. ⊕

Figure 1.1
Number of Community Colleges: 1901–2004

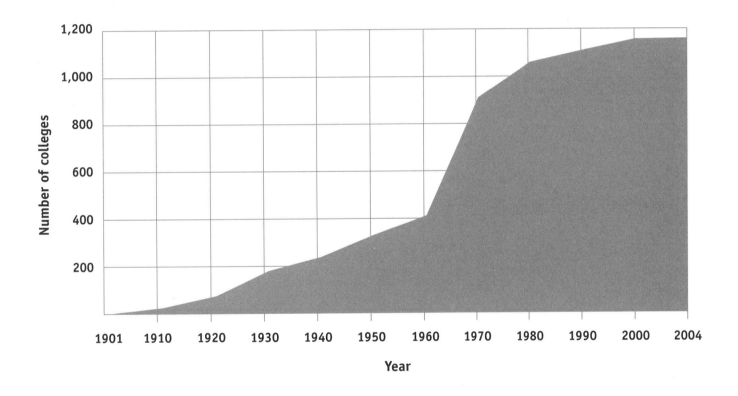

Source: AACC (2004b)

Table 1.1
Number of Community Colleges: 1901–2004

Year	# of Colleges
1901	1
1910	25
1920	74
1930	180
1940	238
1950	330
1960	412
1970	909
1980	1,058
1990	1,108
2000	1,155
2004	1,158

Source: AACC (2004b)

Table 1.2
Number of Community Colleges by State: 2004

State	Private	Public	Tribal	Total	State	Private	Public	Tribal	Total
Alabama	1	23		24	Nebraska		7	2	9
Alaska		5		5	Nevada	1	4		5
Arizona	1	19	2	22	New Hampshire	3	4		7
Arkansas	1	24		25	New Jersey	2	19		21
California	24	111	1	136	New Mexico		15	3	18
Colorado		15		15	New York	18	43		61
Connecticut	5	12		17	North Carolina	2	59		61
Delaware		3		3	North Dakota		5	5	10
District of Columbia	1			1	Ohio	6	34		40
Florida	3	28		31	Oklahoma		15		15
Georgia	6	37		43	Oregon	1	14		15
Hawaii	3	7		10	Pennsylvania	9	18		27
Idaho		4		4	Rhode Island	1	1		2
Illinois	8	45		53	South Carolina	1	17		18
Indiana	2	3		5	South Dakota	1	4	4	9
Iowa	5	15		20	Tennessee	2	13		15
Kansas	3	22		25	Texas	6	66		72
Kentucky	1	16		17	Utah	1	5		6
Louisiana		11		11	Vermont	2	2		4
Maine	2	8		10	Virginia	2	24		26
Maryland	1	18		19	Washington	1	33	1	35
Massachusetts	9	17		26	West Virginia	1	10		11
Michigan	2	28	2	32	Wisconsin		17	2	19
Minnesota	3	28	2	33	Wyoming		7		7
Mississippi		16		16	Outlying Territories	2	6		8
Missouri	5	14		19	Total	148	979	31	1,158
Montana		8	7	15					

Source: AACC (2004b)

Figure 1.2
Location of Community Colleges

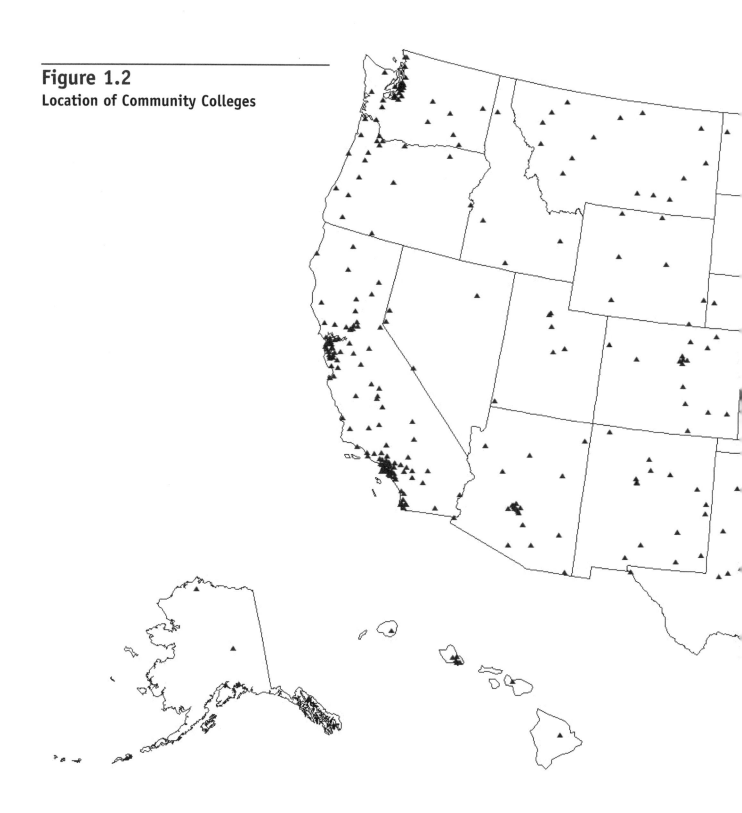

Table 1.3
Undergraduate Enrollment: Fall 2001 and Full Year 2001–2002

Community Colleges			
College Type	Fall 2001	Full year 2001–2002	Fall as a % of full year
Public	6,097,454	9,937,952	61.4%
Independent	134,383	195,922	68.6%
Total	6,231,837	10,133,874	61.5%

4-Year Colleges			
College Type	Fall 2001	Full year 2001–2002	Fall as a % of full year
Public	4,962,705	5,816,865	85.3%
Independent	2,671,851	3,051,839	87.5%
Total	7,634,556	8,868,704	86.1%

Source: NCES (2004e, 2004h)

Figure 1.3

Percentage of U.S. Population Aged 18 or Older Served by Community Colleges: 2001–2002

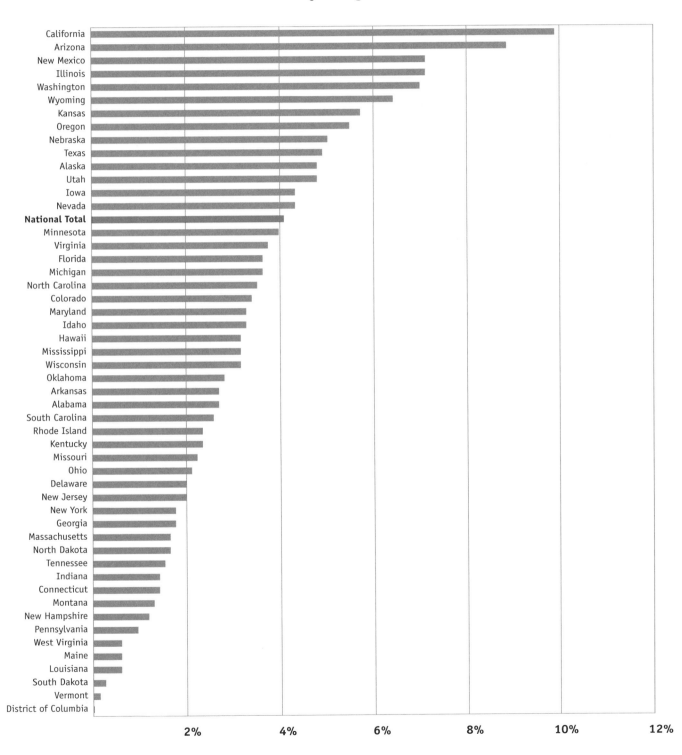

Source: NCES (2004h); U.S. Census Bureau (2004b)

Table 1.4

Percentage of U.S. Population Aged 18 or Older Served by Community Colleges: Fall 2001 and Full Year 2001–2002

State	# Served			Population aged 18 or older	% Served		Rank
	Fall 2001	Full year 2001–2002	Fall as a % of full-year enrollment		% of population served fall 2001	% of population served 2001–2002	
Alabama	76,500	119,583	64.0%	3,355,089	2.3%	3.6%	28
Alaska	11,736	23,934	49.0%	443,064	2.6%	5.4%	11
Arizona	185,039	344,333	53.7%	3,861,087	4.8%	8.9%	2
Arkansas	45,401	72,423	62.7%	2,011,990	2.3%	3.6%	27
California	1,481,850	2,460,008	60.2%	25,177,335	5.9%	9.8%	1
Colorado	79,220	137,236	57.7%	3,291,814	2.4%	4.2%	20
Connecticut	44,148	64,068	68.9%	2,593,471	1.7%	2.5%	42
Delaware	12,291	18,224	67.4%	604,636	2.0%	3.0%	34
District of Columbia	—	—	—	460,873	0.0%	0.0%	51
Florida	345,619	551,038	62.7%	12,568,154	2.7%	4.4%	17
Georgia	108,313	171,884	63.0%	6,162,187	1.8%	2.8%	37
Hawaii	25,969	37,632	69.0%	931,428	2.8%	4.0%	23
Idaho	27,014	39,029	69.2%	950,204	2.8%	4.1%	22
Illinois	345,475	684,062	50.5%	9,272,276	3.7%	7.4%	4
Indiana	69,219	112,339	61.6%	4,535,822	1.5%	2.5%	41
Iowa	72,353	111,879	64.7%	2,221,237	3.3%	5.0%	13
Kansas	72,545	124,364	58.3%	1,998,360	3.6%	6.2%	7
Kentucky	69,762	101,986	68.4%	3,079,098	2.3%	3.3%	31
Louisiana	33,169	57,301	57.9%	3,268,183	1.0%	1.8%	48
Maine	12,905	17,816	72.4%	991,471	1.3%	1.8%	47
Maryland	109,848	165,221	66.5%	4,017,277	2.7%	4.1%	21
Massachusetts	90,301	134,645	67.1%	4,925,984	1.8%	2.7%	38
Michigan	201,407	324,624	62.0%	7,433,782	2.7%	4.4%	18
Minnesota	130,189	175,543	74.2%	3,717,580	3.5%	4.7%	15
Mississippi	60,376	84,397	71.5%	2,094,765	2.9%	4.0%	24
Missouri	85,021	134,227	63.3%	4,229,728	2.0%	3.2%	32
Montana	10,049	16,303	61.6%	685,747	1.5%	2.4%	43

	# Served				% Served		
State	Fall 2001	Full year 2001–2002	Fall as a % of full-year enrollment	Population aged 18 or older	% of population served fall 2001	% of population served 2001–2002	Rank
Nebraska	36,117	71,547	50.5%	1,276,129	2.8%	5.6%	9
Nevada	49,081	77,119	63.6%	1,543,076	3.2%	5.0%	14
New Hampshire	15,063	21,959	68.6%	951,142	1.6%	2.3%	44
New Jersey	132,100	189,285	69.8%	6,396,274	2.1%	3.0%	35
New Mexico	54,599	97,995	55.7%	1,328,276	4.1%	7.4%	3
New York	285,695	407,357	70.1%	14,441,533	2.0%	2.8%	36
North Carolina	181,629	262,416	69.2%	6,171,175	2.9%	4.3%	19
North Dakota	9,098	13,223	68.8%	485,091	1.9%	2.7%	39
Ohio	176,741	268,356	65.9%	8,537,248	2.1%	3.1%	33
Oklahoma	61,461	94,800	64.8%	2,588,799	2.4%	3.7%	26
Oregon	87,208	157,877	55.2%	2,618,763	3.3%	6.0%	8
Pennsylvania	132,749	201,656	65.8%	9,418,495	1.4%	2.1%	45
Rhode Island	18,372	27,102	67.8%	814,451	2.3%	3.3%	30
South Carolina	71,956	106,055	67.8%	3,046,567	2.4%	3.5%	29
South Dakota	6,865	8,300	82.7%	560,348	1.2%	1.5%	49
Tennessee	77,230	112,660	68.6%	4,348,929	1.8%	2.6%	40
Texas	487,502	843,088	57.8%	15,302,983	3.2%	5.5%	10
Utah	55,377	83,492	66.3%	1,549,836	3.6%	5.4%	12
Vermont	6,209	6,629	93.7%	471,443	1.3%	1.4%	50
Virginia	149,939	242,740	61.8%	5,433,719	2.8%	4.5%	16
Washington	184,899	325,831	56.7%	4,483,340	4.1%	7.3%	5
West Virginia	18,890	25,272	74.7%	1,406,199	1.3%	1.8%	46
Wisconsin	109,376	161,692	67.6%	4,064,317	2.7%	4.0%	25
Wyoming	17,179	25,269	68.0%	369,486	4.6%	6.8%	6
Outlying Territories	15,575	18,055	86.3%	—	—	—	—
Total	6,246,629	10,133,874	61.6%	212,490,261	2.9%	4.8%	

Source: NCES (2004e, 2004h)

Figure 1.4
Enrollment at Community Colleges: Fall 2002

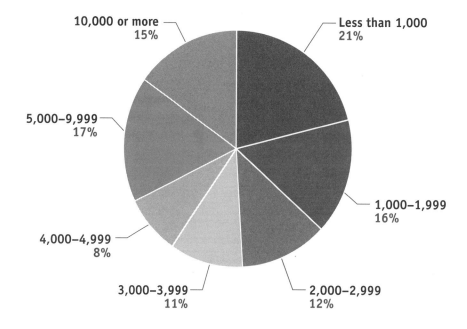

10,000 or more
15%

Less than 1,000
21%

5,000–9,999
17%

1,000–1,999
16%

4,000–4,999
8%

3,000–3,999
11%

2,000–2,999
12%

Source: NCES (2004e)

Figure 1.5
**Percentage Distribution of Community Colleges
by Enrollment: 2002**

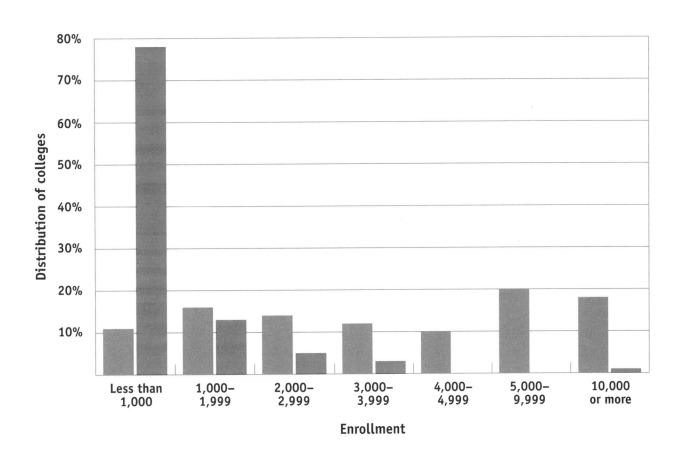

Source: NCES (2004e)

Figure 1.6
Distribution of Community Colleges by Urbanicity: 2002

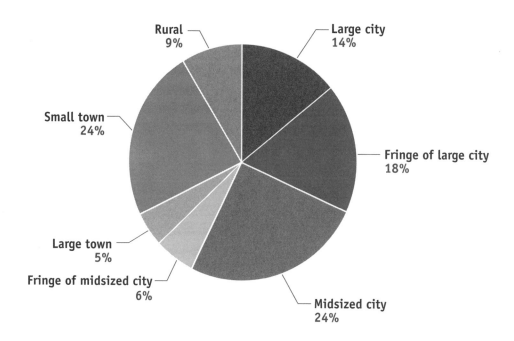

Source: NCES (2004h)

II
Community College Enrollment

Community colleges continue to be seen as the portal to opportunity in the United States, offering high-quality education programs and services that meet the needs of an increasingly diverse national population. Whether students enroll for a few courses or a full-degree program, they expect to leave with the knowledge and skills needed for effective participation in the workforce and civic life of this country. For those who aspire to a higher standard of living, community colleges are truly an open door.

The reasons for choosing to attend these community colleges are as diverse as the students themselves: ease of access, low cost, excellent academic programs that meet learners' and employers' needs, a broad array of support services, proximity to students' homes, flexibility of scheduling, a welcoming campus environment, and links to other levels of education. And, in an era when most jobs require at least some college education and most people can expect to work outside the home for

a major portion of their lives, the decision to attend college is not a luxury but a necessity. For more than 6.5 million students taking courses for credit each fall, these institutions have become the colleges of choice.

The aspirations of these students are equally varied. Some seek career-focused degrees that will allow them to enter or move upward in the job market. Others plan to transfer to institutions offering bachelor's degrees after one or two years of study. Some are broadening their array of job skills by taking a set of courses or another degree in a specialized area so they can be more competitive in the workforce. A growing number of students already have degrees (associate, bachelor's, master's, and higher degrees) and are coming to community colleges for specific job skills that will help them change careers or advance in their current careers. Newly arrived immigrants look to community colleges as a place to learn English and gain job skills. Still others enroll for enrichment courses in the arts, new technologies, or other areas of interest.

Ease of access and low cost are often the factors that first draw students to community college campuses. Even if they decide to enroll at the last moment, students generally can gain entry to the college, although specific academic programs may have selective admissions. Based on skills assessments and counseling at the point of initial enrollment, they are able to design a program of study that meets their education goals and life circumstances.

Recent national surveys confirm that cost is the primary concern of most college students. Many of them are financially independent, working full or part time and supporting families while enrolled. (Community College Survey, 2002; NCES, 1996). The low tuition at community colleges, combined with the possibility of financial aid, makes postsecondary education an option for many who otherwise could not attend college because they lack the financial resources. For low-income families, these colleges provide a way to escape the cycle of poverty.

Community colleges also offer many families a means to reduce the total cost of a baccalaureate education by keeping expenses low for the first two years and making the transition easier through articulation agreements with four-year institutions. Furthermore, the presence of a community college within driving distance of most people's homes allows students to avoid the expenses associated with residential campuses. Community colleges provide an excellent alternative to four-year and for-profit institutions.

Currently, the average age of community college students is 29. (NCES, 2004j;) This is probably caused primarily by an increase in the number of traditional-age students (17–21) attending community colleges. The lower tuition at community colleges, along with cost savings from staying at home, are incentives for many students and families of the baby boom generation.

Since 1985, more than half of all community college students have been women. Many of these women are in their mid- to late twenties, attend part time, have children, and have chosen to return to school so they can gain skills to help support their families. Easy access and low cost are compelling factors in their decision to enroll. Other attractions are the existence of support services such as tutoring and campus-based child care at many of the colleges, as

well as the close proximity of campuses to their homes. Also, because some of these female students are unsure about their ability to succeed academically, the nonthreatening learning-centered campus environment allows them to make a comfortable transition into college.

Students of color have found community colleges to be an excellent entry point into higher education. At present, the majority of Black and Hispanic students in this country begin their postsecondary studies at these colleges. Low tuition is certainly an important factor, and the greater diversity of the student population may help minorities—who are often the first in their families to attend college—feel at home on campus. Many colleges offer targeted services for these students, including English language studies, social activities, and articulation agreements with historically Black colleges and universities (HBCUs). At least seven community colleges, primarily in the South, are HBCUs. For students of color, like female students, close proximity to home and flexible course schedules at two-year colleges help them meet family and job obligations and maintain links to their communities.

About 33% of all community college students are minorities, and that proportion is expected to rise as the American population becomes

increasingly diverse. This contingent of minority students includes a growing number of Asian Americans and a small population enrolled at tribal colleges established specifically to meet the education needs of Native Americans. One noteworthy development over the past few years has been an increase in the number of colleges designated by the federal government as Hispanic-serving institutions (HSIs), that is, colleges with more than 25% Hispanic student enrollment. Particularly in the Southwest and West, the number of HSIs that are community colleges is expected to increase dramatically in the next few years.

The comprehensive mission of most community colleges makes them attractive to a broad range of people who seek particular programs or opportunities. Many teens accelerate their studies by taking college courses while in high school through dual-enrollment and advanced placement options, thus saving substantially on the cost of education. High-performing students can participate in honors programs; the community college honors society, Phi Theta Kappa; and student leadership programs. Students who lack the skills for college study can begin with developmental education and English as a second language courses. Baccalaureate holders can return to study new areas or expand their job skills. People with disabilities can enroll at these readily accessible campuses and succeed academically with the aid of special support services. Foreign students can take advantage of America's superior higher education system and make a transition to life in the United States or apply their advanced learning in their home countries after graduation. Senior citizens can take credit and noncredit courses and engage in cultural activities or even attain the college degree they were unable to earn in their earlier years. The newest population of learners, those who choose to study through distance education, has also found a home in these colleges via the Internet. All of these groups enrich the learning environment on community college campuses.

An important component in the mission of these institutions is to develop the human capital that makes this country a powerful global economic force. To that end, community colleges work closely with business and industry to offer for-credit and noncredit programs focused on workforce development. New academic programs are continually being created and existing programs are fine-tuned to meet changing market needs. As new career fields such as cybersecurity, nanotechnology, agriscience, and biotechnology and health-care professionals who special-

ize in these fields emerge, community colleges are able to respond rapidly with degree programs, certificates, and customized training. People seeking to enter existing fields where the demand for workers is growing—such as health care, retailing, and human services—can gain skills at their local college and move quickly into jobs.

With a highly diverse student body characterized by differing aspirations, life circumstances, and skill levels, community colleges are challenged to provide learning experiences and support services that meet the needs of distinct groups. They must also be accountable for the outcomes of their programs and services, ensuring that all students accomplish their education goals and can demonstrate real learning that can be applied in work and life settings. The challenge is particularly difficult when serving students who are considered to be at high risk—students who are academically underprepared, burdened with family responsibilities, working more than 30 hours per week, studying part time, and lacking financial resources. They may have less ambitious aspirations and are more likely to drop out or pause. Fortunately, the array of services available at community colleges and the greater levels of individual attention make it possible for high-risk students to persist in their studies, complete

degrees, and move on to higher levels of study or entry-level jobs.

Whatever the aspirations and preparation levels of students who enroll, they will find that community colleges offer a dynamic, learning-centered environment that fosters success. In colleges that are making the transition to the learning college model, faculty have developed new instructional approaches that produce measurable learning outcomes, and staff have strengthened the support services that help students achieve their academic goals. These colleges have become vibrant learning communities where students, faculty, and staff work collaboratively to learn and grow.

As the United States has moved from providing higher education primarily to the most privileged members of its population to one that provides opportunities to all members of the population, community colleges have come to the forefront, welcoming all those who aspire to advanced learning. In partnership with schools, businesses, and other organizations in their local areas, community colleges provide opportunities for learning over a lifetime. With enrollments at degree-granting institutions projected to grow by 20% in the next 10 years, community colleges—the people's colleges—will continue to be a vital part of American life and learning. ⊕

Figure 2.1
Undergraduate and Graduate Enrollment: 1965–2001

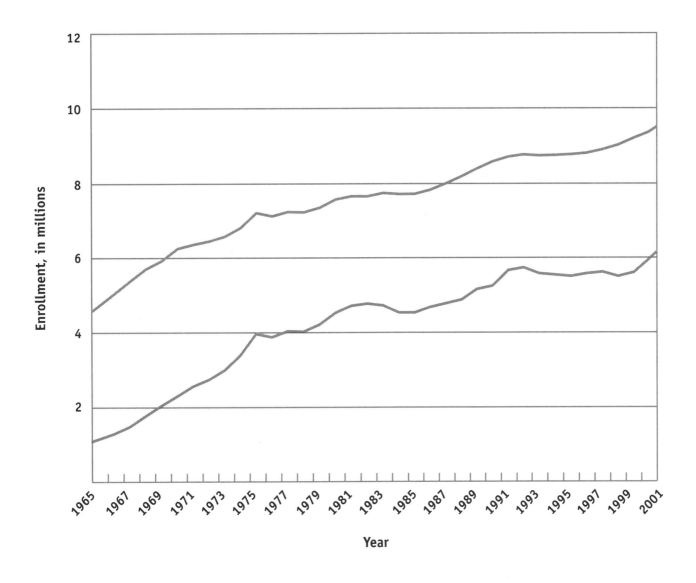

Source: Snyder (2003)

Note. Data are based on the U.S. Department of Education definition of community colleges (see Glossary).

Table 2.1
Undergraduate and Graduate Enrollment: 1965–2001

Year	Community Colleges			4-Year Colleges			
	Public	Independent	Total	Public	Independent	Total	Grand Total
1965[a]	1,041,264	131,688	1,172,952	2,928,332	1,819,580	4,747,912	5,920,864
1966[a]	1,189,169	136,801	1,325,970	3,159,748	1,904,154	5,063,902	6,389,872
1967[a]	1,372,053	140,709	1,512,762	3,443,975	1,955,011	5,398,986	6,911,748
1968[a]	1,646,474	145,822	1,792,296	3,784,178	1,936,617	5,720,795	7,513,091
1969	1,934,346	133,187	2,067,533	3,962,522	1,974,605	5,937,127	8,004,660
1970	2,195,412	123,973	2,319,385	4,232,722	2,028,780	6,261,502	8,580,887
1971	2,457,319	121,970	2,579,289	4,346,990	2,022,365	6,369,355	8,948,644
1972	2,640,939	115,247	2,756,186	4,429,696	2,028,938	6,458,634	9,214,820
1973	2,889,621	122,479	3,012,100	4,529,895	2,060,128	6,590,023	9,602,123
1974	3,285,482	118,512	3,403,994	4,703,018	2,116,717	6,819,735	10,223,729
1975	3,836,366	133,753	3,970,119	4,998,142	2,216,598	7,214,740	11,184,859
1976	3,751,786	131,535	3,883,321	4,901,691	2,227,125	7,128,816	11,012,137
1977	3,901,769	141,173	4,042,942	4,945,224	2,297,621	7,242,845	11,285,787
1978	3,873,690	154,777	4,028,467	4,912,203	2,319,422	7,231,625	11,260,092
1979	4,056,810	159,856	4,216,666	4,980,012	2,373,221	7,353,233	11,569,899
1980	4,328,782	197,505	4,526,287	5,128,612	2,441,996	7,570,608	12,096,895
1981	4,480,708	235,503	4,716,211	5,166,324	2,489,137	7,655,461	12,371,672
1982	4,519,653	252,053	4,771,706	5,176,434	2,477,640	7,654,074	12,425,780
1983	4,459,330	264,136	4,723,466	5,223,404	2,517,791	7,741,195	12,464,661
1984	4,279,097	251,676	4,530,773	5,198,273	2,512,894	7,711,167	12,241,940
1985	4,269,733	261,344	4,531,077	5,209,540	2,506,438	7,715,978	12,247,055
1986	4,413,691	265,857	4,679,548	5,300,202	2,523,761	7,823,963	12,503,511
1987	4,541,054	235,168	4,776,222	5,432,200	2,558,220	7,990,420	12,766,642
1988	4,615,487	259,668	4,875,155	5,545,901	2,634,281	8,180,182	13,055,337
1989	4,883,660	267,229	5,150,889	5,694,303	2,693,368	8,387,671	13,538,560
1990	4,996,475	243,608	5,240,083	5,848,242	2,730,312	8,578,554	13,818,637
1991	5,404,815	247,085	5,651,900	5,904,748	2,802,305	8,707,053	14,358,953

	Community Colleges			4-Year Colleges			
Year	Public	Independent	Total	Public	Independent	Total	Grand Total
1992	5,484,555	237,835	5,722,390	5,900,012	2,864,957	8,764,969	14,487,359
1993	5,337,328	228,539	5,565,867	5,851,760	2,887,176	8,738,936	14,304,803
1994	5,308,467	221,243	5,529,710	5,825,213	2,923,867	8,749,080	14,278,790
1995	5,277,829	214,700	5,492,529	5,814,545	2,954,707	8,769,252	14,261,781
1996	5,314,463	248,864	5,563,327	5,806,036	2,998,157	8,804,193	14,367,520
1997	5,360,686	244,883	5,605,569	5,835,433	3,061,332	8,896,765	14,502,334
1998	5,245,963	243,351	5,489,314	5,891,806	3,125,847	9,017,653	14,506,967
1999	5,339,449	253,250	5,592,699	5,969,950	3,228,575	9,198,525	14,791,224
2000	5,697,388	251,043	5,948,431	6,055,398	3,308,460	9,363,858	15,312,289
2001	5,996,701	253,878	6,250,579	6,236,455	3,440,953	9,677,408	15,927,987
Change 1965–1971	136.0%	-5.9%	97.7%	44.5%	11.5%	31.9%	44.9%
Change 1971–1981	82.3%	93.1%	82.8%	18.8%	23.1%	20.2%	38.3%
Change 1981–1991	20.6%	4.9%	19.8%	14.3%	12.6%	13.7%	16.1%
Change 1991–2001	11.0%	2.7%	10.6%	5.6%	22.8%	11.1%	10.9%
Change 1965–2001	475.9%	92.8%	432.9%	113.0%	89.1%	103.8%	169.0%

Source: Snyder (2003)

Note. Data are based on the U.S. Department of Education definition of community colleges (see Glossary).

[a]Data for community college branch campuses of 4-year colleges are included with the 4-year colleges.

Table 2.2
Undergraduate Fall Enrollment: 1993–2002

Year	Community Colleges			4-Year Colleges			Grand Total
	Public	Independent	Total	Public	Independent	Total	
1993	5,450,395	130,465	5,580,860	4,656,882	2,294,001	6,950,883	12,531,743
1994	5,434,265	127,211	5,561,476	4,603,818	2,295,465	6,899,283	12,460,759
1995	5,349,385	126,576	5,475,961	4,612,236	2,314,091	6,926,327	12,402,288
1996	5,381,112	127,111	5,508,223	4,597,086	2,332,324	6,929,410	12,437,633
1997	5,407,886	130,092	5,537,978	4,619,671	2,312,213	6,931,884	12,469,862
1998	5,397,934	135,449	5,533,383	4,677,908	2,436,049	7,113,957	12,647,340
1999	5,446,613	126,785	5,573,398	4,716,552	2,469,520	7,186,072	12,759,470
2000	5,812,042	130,329	5,942,371	4,798,961	2,557,797	7,356,758	13,299,129
2001	6,097,454	134,383	6,231,837	4,962,705	2,671,851	7,634,556	13,866,393
2002	6,417,269	145,117	6,562,386	5,091,050	2,762,638	7,853,688	14,416,074
Change 1993–1998	-1.0%	3.8%	-0.9%	0.5%	6.2%	2.3%	0.9%
Change 1998–2002	18.9%	7.1%	18.6%	8.8%	13.4%	10.4%	14.0%
Change 1993–2002	17.7%	11.2%	17.6%	9.3%	20.4%	13.0%	15.0%

Source: NCES (2004e)

Figure 2.2
**Undergraduate Enrollment: Fall 2001 and
Full Year 2001–2002**

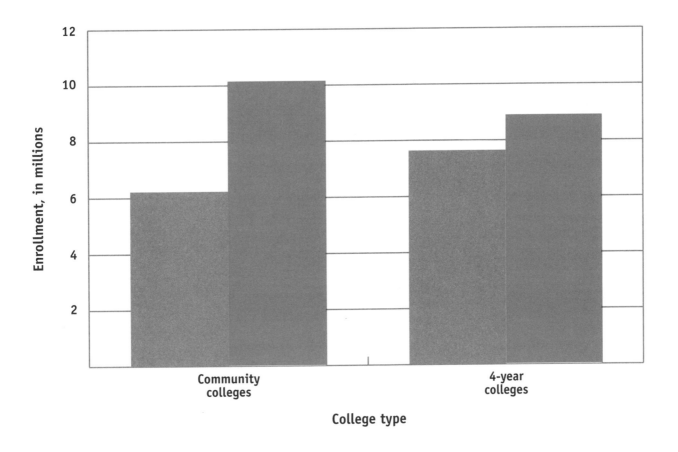

Legend:
■ Fall 2001
■ Full year, 2001–2002

Source: NCES (2004e, 2004h)

Table 2.3

Undergraduate Fall Enrollment by Attendance Status and Gender: 1993–2002

Attendance Status and Gender	Community Colleges			4-Year Colleges		
	Public	Independent	Total	Public	Independent	Total
1993						
Enrolled full time	1,945,383	97,963	2,043,346	3,523,655	1,730,872	5,254,527
Enrolled part time	3,505,012	32,502	3,537,514	1,133,227	563,129	1,696,356
% part time	64.3%	24.9%	63.4%	24.3%	24.5%	24.4%
Men	2,301,563	48,425	2,349,988	2,192,611	1,031,969	3,224,580
Women	3,148,832	82,040	3,230,872	2,464,271	1,262,032	3,726,303
% women	57.8%	62.9%	57.9%	52.9%	55.0%	53.6%
Total	5,450,395	130,465	5,580,860	4,656,882	2,294,001	6,950,883
1994						
Enrolled full time	1,962,057	96,240	2,058,297	3,507,009	1,745,795	5,252,804
Enrolled part time	3,472,208	30,971	3,503,179	1,096,809	549,670	1,646,479
% part time	63.9%	24.3%	63.0%	23.8%	23.9%	23.9%
Men	2,286,357	47,303	2,333,660	2,148,006	1,021,959	3,169,965
Women	3,147,908	79,908	3,227,816	2,455,812	1,273,506	3,729,318
% women	57.9%	62.8%	58.0%	53.3%	55.5%	54.1%
Total	5,434,265	127,211	5,561,476	4,603,818	2,295,465	6,899,283
1995						
Enrolled full time	1,923,171	96,473	2,019,644	3,529,783	1,758,164	5,287,947
Enrolled part time	3,426,214	30,103	3,456,317	1,082,453	555,927	1,638,380
% part time	64.0%	23.8%	63.1%	23.5%	24.0%	23.7%
Men	2,245,429	46,644	2,292,073	2,130,861	1,018,214	3,149,075
Women	3,103,956	79,932	3,183,888	2,481,375	1,295,877	3,777,252
% women	58.0%	63.1%	58.1%	53.8%	56.0%	54.5%
Total	5,349,385	126,576	5,475,961	4,612,236	2,314,091	6,926,327

Attendance Status and Gender	Community Colleges			4-Year Colleges		
	Public	Independent	Total	Public	Independent	Total
1996						
Enrolled full time	1,945,488	98,674	2,044,162	3,546,207	1,783,675	5,329,882
Enrolled part time	3,435,587	28,474	3,464,061	1,050,879	548,649	1,599,528
% part time	63.8%	22.4%	62.9%	22.9%	23.5%	23.1%
Men	2,263,554	49,045	2,312,599	2,108,371	1,035,936	3,144,307
Women	3,117,521	78,103	3,195,624	2,488,715	1,296,388	3,785,103
% women	57.9%	61.4%	58.0%	54.1%	55.6%	54.6%
Total	5,381,075	127,148	5,508,223	4,597,086	2,332,324	6,929,410
1997						
Enrolled full time	1,960,742	101,023	2,061,765	3,598,019	1,811,076	5,409,095
Enrolled part time	3,447,144	29,069	3,476,213	1,021,652	501,137	1,522,789
% part time	63.7%	22.3%	62.8%	22.1%	21.7%	22.0%
Men	2,282,305	52,248	2,334,553	2,103,500	1,009,590	3,113,090
Women	3,125,581	77,844	3,203,425	2,516,171	1,302,623	3,818,794
% women	57.8%	59.8%	57.8%	54.5%	56.3%	55.1%
Total	5,407,886	130,092	5,537,978	4,619,671	2,312,213	6,931,884
1998						
Enrolled full time	1,965,884	103,227	2,069,111	3,648,944	1,955,237	5,604,181
Enrolled part time	3,432,050	32,222	3,464,272	1,028,964	480,812	1,509,776
% part time	63.6%	23.8%	62.6%	22.0%	19.7%	21.2%
Men	2,295,059	54,851	2,349,910	2,112,727	1,061,055	3,173,782
Women	3,102,875	80,598	3,183,473	2,565,181	1,374,994	3,940,175
% women	57.5%	59.5%	57.5%	54.8%	56.4%	55.4%
Total	5,397,934	135,449	5,533,383	4,677,908	2,436,049	7,113,957

Table 2.3 (cont'd)

Undergraduate Fall Enrollment by Attendance Status and Gender: 1993–2002

Attendance Status and Gender	Community Colleges			4-Year Colleges		
	Public	Independent	Total	Public	Independent	Total
1999						
Enrolled full time	2,000,219	97,290	2,097,509	3,698,691	1,992,007	5,690,698
Enrolled part time	3,446,394	29,495	3,475,889	1,017,861	477,513	1,495,374
% part time	63.3%	23.3%	62.4%	21.6%	19.3%	20.8%
Men	2,325,023	52,971	2,377,994	2,124,546	1,080,651	3,205,197
Women	3,121,590	73,814	3,195,404	2,592,006	1,388,869	3,980,875
% women	57.3%	58.2%	57.3%	55.0%	56.2%	55.4%
Total	5,446,613	126,785	5,573,398	4,716,552	2,469,520	7,186,072
2000						
Enrolled full time	2,071,643	101,014	2,172,657	3,772,041	2,078,945	5,850,986
Enrolled part time	3,740,399	29,315	3,769,714	1,026,920	478,852	1,505,772
% part time	64.4%	22.5%	63.4%	21.4%	18.7%	20.5%
Men	2,496,709	55,870	2,552,579	2,151,133	1,125,938	3,277,071
Women	3,315,333	74,459	3,389,792	2,647,828	1,431,859	4,079,687
% women	57.0%	57.1%	57.0%	55.2%	56.0%	55.5%
Total	5,812,042	130,329	5,942,371	4,798,961	2,557,797	7,356,758
2001						
Enrolled full time	2,225,445	107,000	2,332,445	3,919,363	2,190,672	6,110,035
Enrolled part time	3,872,009	27,383	3,899,392	1,043,342	481,179	1,524,521
% part time	63.5%	20.4%	62.6%	21.0%	18.0%	20.0%
Men	2,603,313	56,652	2,659,965	2,223,843	1,170,482	3,394,325
Women	3,494,141	77,731	3,571,872	2,738,862	1,501,369	4,240,231
% women	57.3%	57.8%	57.3%	55.2%	56.2%	55.5%
Total	6,097,454	134,383	6,231,837	4,962,705	2,671,851	7,634,556
2002						
Enrolled full time	2,423,384	112,759	2,536,143	4,046,191	2,263,598	6,309,789
Enrolled part time	3,993,885	32,358	4,026,243	1,044,859	499,040	1,543,899
% part time	62.2%	22.3%	61.4%	20.5%	18.1%	19.7%
Men	2,704,592	59,857	2,764,449	2,279,557	1,203,953	3,483,510
Women	3,712,677	85,260	3,797,937	2,811,493	1,558,685	4,370,178
% women	57.9%	58.8%	57.9%	55.2%	56.4%	55.6%
Total	6,417,269	145,117	6,562,386	5,091,050	2,762,638	7,853,688

Source: NCES (2004e)

Figure 2.3

Age Distribution of Community College Students: Biennually, 1993–2001

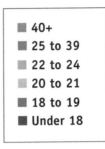

- 40+
- 25 to 39
- 22 to 24
- 20 to 21
- 18 to 19
- Under 18

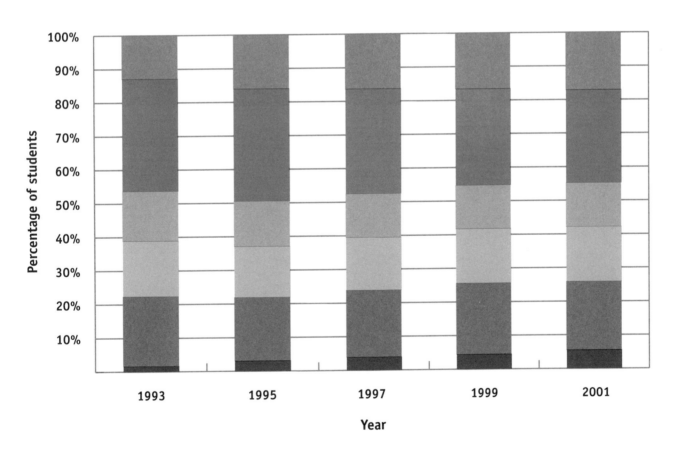

Source: NCES (2004e)

Table 2.4

Distribution of Community College Fall Enrollment by Age and Attendance Status: Biennually, 1993–2001

Age	Enrolled Part Time			Enrolled Full Time			All Students		
	Public	Independent	Total	Public	Independent	Total	Public	Independent	Total
1993									
Under 18	1.6%	0.9%	1.6%	1.6%	2.5%	1.7%	1.6%	2.1%	1.6%
18–19	10.3%	6.3%	10.3%	35.3%	35.8%	35.4%	20.6%	29.7%	20.8%
20–21	12.8%	11.9%	12.7%	21.5%	18.9%	21.4%	16.3%	17.5%	16.4%
22–24	15.6%	15.8%	15.6%	13.7%	13.3%	13.7%	14.8%	13.8%	14.8%
25–29	17.1%	17.8%	17.1%	10.1%	10.2%	10.1%	14.2%	11.7%	14.2%
30–34	13.9%	14.8%	13.9%	6.8%	6.0%	6.7%	11.0%	7.8%	10.9%
35–39	11.1%	11.9%	11.1%	4.7%	4.1%	4.7%	8.5%	5.7%	8.4%
40–49	12.3%	11.9%	12.3%	4.6%	3.6%	4.5%	9.1%	5.3%	9.0%
50–64	3.7%	2.6%	3.7%	0.9%	0.8%	0.9%	2.6%	1.2%	2.5%
65 or older	0.9%	0.1%	0.9%	0.1%	0.0%	0.1%	0.6%	0.1%	0.6%
Age unknown	0.7%	6.0%	0.8%	0.6%	4.8%	0.8%	0.7%	5.0%	0.8%
1995									
Under 18	3.6%	2.3%	3.6%	2.1%	1.8%	2.1%	3.1%	1.9%	3.1%
18–19	9.4%	6.2%	9.4%	35.7%	34.3%	35.6%	18.7%	27.9%	18.9%
20–21	11.2%	10.7%	11.2%	21.8%	19.9%	21.7%	15.0%	17.8%	15.0%
22–24	13.6%	14.3%	13.7%	13.1%	14.5%	13.1%	13.4%	14.5%	13.5%
25–29	16.5%	18.4%	16.5%	10.3%	11.7%	10.4%	14.3%	13.2%	14.3%
30–34	13.0%	14.4%	13.0%	6.2%	6.5%	6.2%	10.6%	8.3%	10.6%
35–39	11.0%	12.3%	11.1%	4.5%	4.5%	4.5%	8.7%	6.3%	8.7%
40–49	14.0%	13.9%	14.0%	4.7%	4.2%	4.7%	10.7%	6.4%	10.6%
50–64	5.0%	3.6%	5.0%	1.1%	1.0%	1.1%	3.6%	1.6%	3.6%
65 or older	1.6%	0.4%	1.6%	0.2%	0.1%	0.2%	1.1%	0.2%	1.1%
Age unknown	1.0%	3.5%	1.0%	0.3%	1.5%	0.4%	0.7%	1.9%	0.8%

Source: NCES (2004e)

Age	Enrolled Part Time			Enrolled Full Time			All Students		
	Public	Independent	Total	Public	Independent	Total	Public	Independent	Total
1997									
Under 18	4.9%	2.5%	4.9%	2.2%	1.7%	2.2%	3.9%	1.9%	3.9%
18–19	9.7%	9.0%	9.7%	37.3%	34.1%	37.1%	19.7%	28.3%	19.9%
20–21	11.4%	10.9%	11.4%	22.7%	19.3%	22.6%	15.5%	17.4%	15.6%
22–24	13.2%	13.9%	13.2%	12.6%	14.2%	12.6%	12.9%	14.1%	13.0%
25–29	16.1%	18.0%	16.1%	9.9%	12.0%	10.0%	13.9%	13.3%	13.8%
30–34	11.8%	13.2%	11.8%	5.3%	6.4%	5.4%	9.5%	7.9%	9.4%
35–39	10.4%	11.4%	10.4%	3.9%	4.3%	4.0%	8.1%	5.9%	8.0%
40–49	14.1%	13.8%	14.1%	4.4%	4.1%	4.4%	10.6%	6.3%	10.5%
50–64	5.7%	4.0%	5.6%	1.1%	1.1%	1.1%	4.0%	1.7%	4.0%
65 or older	1.7%	0.3%	1.7%	0.1%	0.1%	0.1%	1.1%	0.1%	1.1%
Age unknown	1.0%	3.1%	1.0%	0.4%	2.8%	0.5%	0.8%	2.8%	0.8%
1999									
Under 18	5.8%	3.0%	5.8%	2.3%	1.6%	2.3%	4.5%	1.9%	4.4%
18–19	10.8%	7.1%	10.8%	38.7%	34.6%	38.5%	21.1%	28.4%	21.2%
20–21	11.9%	11.9%	11.9%	23.0%	20.5%	22.9%	16.0%	18.6%	16.1%
22–24	13.3%	14.1%	13.3%	12.2%	13.7%	12.3%	12.9%	13.8%	12.9%
25–29	15.0%	17.4%	15.0%	9.1%	10.6%	9.1%	12.8%	12.1%	12.8%
30–34	10.8%	12.4%	10.8%	4.8%	5.5%	4.8%	8.6%	7.0%	8.5%
35–39	9.8%	10.6%	9.8%	3.7%	3.8%	3.7%	7.6%	5.4%	7.5%
40–49	13.7%	13.9%	13.7%	4.1%	3.8%	4.1%	10.2%	6.1%	10.1%
50–64	6.0%	3.9%	6.0%	1.2%	1.0%	1.2%	4.2%	1.7%	4.2%
65 or older	1.6%	0.2%	1.6%	0.1%	0.1%	0.1%	1.1%	0.1%	1.0%
Age unknown	1.4%	5.4%	1.4%	0.9%	4.6%	1.0%	1.2%	4.8%	1.3%
2001									
Under 18	7.3%	3.4%	7.3%	2.4%	1.4%	2.4%	5.6%	1.8%	5.5%
18–19	10.4%	7.4%	10.3%	37.4%	30.4%	37.1%	20.2%	25.5%	20.4%
20–21	11.8%	11.1%	11.8%	23.6%	21.3%	23.5%	16.1%	19.1%	16.2%
22–24	13.1%	14.9%	13.1%	12.6%	15.6%	12.7%	12.9%	15.5%	13.0%
25–29	14.0%	17.1%	14.1%	9.0%	11.3%	9.1%	12.2%	12.5%	12.2%
30–34	10.8%	13.0%	10.8%	5.1%	6.1%	5.2%	8.7%	7.6%	8.7%
35–39	8.9%	10.1%	9.0%	3.4%	3.8%	3.4%	6.9%	5.1%	6.9%
40–49	13.5%	14.1%	13.5%	4.1%	4.1%	4.1%	10.1%	6.2%	10.0%
50– 64	6.5%	4.3%	6.5%	1.2%	1.1%	1.2%	4.6%	1.7%	4.5%
65 or older	1.7%	0.3%	1.7%	0.1%	0.1%	0.1%	1.1%	0.1%	1.1%
Age unknown	1.9%	4.1%	1.9%	1.0%	4.9%	1.1%	1.5%	4.8%	1.6%

Table 2.5

Community College Enrollment by Gender, Age, and Attendance Status: Fall 2001

Age	Men Full time	Men Part time	Men % part time	Women Full time	Women Part time	Women % part time	Total Full time	Total Part time	Total % part time
17 or younger	22,630	125,432	84.7%	33,164	159,051	82.7%	55,794	284,483	83.6%
18–19	397,600	184,410	31.7%	466,069	217,765	31.8%	863,669	402,175	31.8%
20–21	265,379	203,877	43.4%	282,945	254,179	47.3%	548,324	458,056	45.5%
22–24	139,656	222,657	61.5%	157,082	286,619	64.6%	296,738	509,276	63.2%
25–29	88,494	231,916	72.4%	124,239	314,476	71.7%	212,733	546,392	72.0%
30–34	44,236	171,610	79.5%	76,289	249,012	76.5%	120,525	420,622	77.7%
35–39	26,489	131,555	83.2%	53,029	216,549	80.3%	79,518	348,104	81.4%
40–49	34,120	186,677	84.5%	62,291	338,202	84.4%	96,411	524,879	84.5%
50–64	11,791	93,660	88.8%	16,735	159,020	90.5%	28,526	252,680	89.9%
65 or older	1,124	25,338	95.8%	1,075	41,295	97.5%	2,199	66,633	96.8%
Unknown	12,413	32,298	72.2%	14,010	41,014	74.5%	26,423	73,312	73.5%
18–21	662,979	388,287	36.9%	749,014	471,944	38.7%	1,411,993	860,231	37.9%
40 or older	47,035	305,675	86.7%	80,101	538,517	87.1%	127,136	844,192	86.9%
Total	1,043,932	1,609,430	60.7%	1,286,928	2,277,182	63.9%	2,330,860	3,886,612	62.5%

Source: NCES (2004e)

Note. Total enrollment by age may vary from other tables because of unreported data.

Table 2.6

Community College Enrollment by Age and Gender: Fall 2001

Age	Gender		
	Men	Women	% women
17 or younger	148,062	192,215	56.5%
18–19	582,010	683,834	54.0%
20–21	469,256	537,124	53.4%
22–24	362,313	443,701	55.0%
25–29	320,410	438,715	57.8%
30–34	215,846	325,301	60.1%
35–39	158,044	269,578	63.0%
40–49	220,797	400,493	64.5%
50–64	105,451	175,755	62.5%
65 or older	26,462	42,370	61.6%
Unknown	44,711	55,024	55.2%
18–21	1,051,266	1,220,958	53.7%
40 or older	352,710	618,618	63.7%
Total	2,653,362	3,564,110	57.3%

Source: NCES (2004e)

Note. Total enrollment by age may vary from other tables because of unreported data.

Table 2.7

Undergraduate Fall Enrollment by Race/Ethnicity: 1993–2002

Race/Ethnicity	Community Colleges			4-Year Colleges			All Colleges			% enrolled in community colleges
	Fall enrollment	% of Total enrollment	% of Minority enrollment	Fall enrollment	% of Total enrollment	% of Minority enrollment	Fall enrollment	% of Total enrollment	% of Minority enrollment	
1993										
Black	568,657	10.2%	38.5%	691,954	10.0%	44.7%	1,260,611	10.1%	41.7%	45.1%
Native American	65,322	1.2%	4.4%	46,327	0.7%	3.0%	111,649	0.9%	3.7%	58.5%
Asian/Pacific Islander	290,580	5.2%	19.7%	325,458	4.7%	21.0%	616,038	4.9%	20.4%	47.2%
Hispanic	551,922	9.9%	37.4%	483,107	7.0%	31.2%	1,035,029	8.3%	34.2%	53.3%
Minority subtotal	1,476,481	26.5%	100.0%	1,546,846	22.3%	100.0%	3,023,327	24.1%	100.0%	48.8%
White, non-Hispanic	3,857,662	69.1%	—	4,991,754	71.8%	—	8,849,416	70.6%	—	43.6%
Race/ethnicity unknown	154,686	2.8%	—	234,952	3.4%	—	389,638	3.1%	—	39.7%
Nonresident alien	92,031	1.6%	—	177,331	2.6%	—	269,362	2.1%	—	34.2%
Total	5,580,860	100.0%	—	6,950,883	100.0%	—	12,531,743	100.0%	—	44.5%
1994										
Black	585,333	10.5%	38.0%	703,837	10.2%	43.9%	1,289,170	10.3%	41.0%	45.4%
Native American	68,310	1.2%	4.4%	48,523	0.7%	3.0%	116,833	0.9%	3.7%	58.5%
Asian/Pacific Islander	308,368	5.5%	20.0%	347,230	5.0%	21.7%	655,598	5.3%	20.9%	47.0%
Hispanic	579,410	10.4%	37.6%	502,937	7.3%	31.4%	1,082,347	8.7%	34.4%	53.5%
Minority subtotal	1,541,421	27.7%	100.0%	1,602,527	23.2%	100.0%	3,143,948	25.2%	100.0%	49.0%
White, non-Hispanic	3,771,591	67.8%	—	4,898,810	71.0%	—	8,670,401	69.6%	—	43.5%
Race/ethnicity unknown	156,416	2.8%	—	219,524	3.2%	—	375,940	3.0%	—	41.6%
Nonresident alien	92,048	1.7%	—	178,422	2.6%	—	270,470	2.2%	—	34.0%
Total	5,561,476	100.0%	—	6,899,283	100.0%	—	12,460,759	100.0%	—	44.6%
1995										
Black	581,176	10.6%	37.2%	710,359	10.3%	42.8%	1,291,535	10.4%	40.1%	45.0%
Native American	70,482	1.3%	4.5%	50,506	0.7%	3.0%	120,988	1.0%	3.8%	58.3%
Asian/Pacific Islander	307,667	5.6%	19.7%	362,589	5.2%	21.9%	670,256	5.4%	20.8%	45.9%
Hispanic	601,423	11.0%	38.5%	534,552	7.7%	32.2%	1,135,975	9.2%	35.3%	52.9%
Minority subtotal	1,560,748	28.5%	100.0%	1,658,006	23.9%	100.0%	3,218,754	26.0%	100.0%	48.5%
White, non-Hispanic	3,654,395	66.7%	—	4,841,184	69.9%	—	8,495,579	68.5%	—	43.0%
Race/ethnicity unknown	170,819	3.1%	—	248,357	3.6%	—	419,176	3.4%	—	40.8%
Nonresident alien	89,999	1.6%	—	178,780	2.6%	—	268,779	2.2%	—	33.5%
Total	5,475,961	100.0%	—	6,926,327	100.0%	—	12,402,288	100.0%	—	44.2%

Race/Ethnicity	Community Colleges			4-Year Colleges			All Colleges			% enrolled in community colleges
	Fall enrollment	% of Total enrollment	Minority enrollment	Fall enrollment	% of Total enrollment	Minority enrollment	Fall enrollment	% of Total enrollment	Minority enrollment	
1996										
Black	593,187	10.8%	36.7%	716,400	10.3%	42.5%	1,309,587	10.5%	39.6%	45.3%
Native American	70,497	1.3%	4.4%	51,583	0.7%	3.1%	122,080	1.0%	3.7%	57.7%
Asian/Pacific Islander	315,550	5.7%	19.5%	373,018	5.4%	22.1%	688,568	5.5%	20.8%	45.8%
Hispanic	636,730	11.6%	39.4%	546,340	7.9%	32.4%	1,183,070	9.5%	35.8%	53.8%
Minority subtotal	1,615,964	29.3%	100.0%	1,687,341	24.4%	100.0%	3,303,305	26.6%	100.0%	48.9%
White, non-Hispanic	3,615,123	65.6%	—	4,791,489	69.1%	—	8,406,612	67.6%	—	43.0%
Race/ethnicity unknown	183,551	3.3%	—	269,087	3.9%	—	452,638	3.6%	—	40.6%
Nonresident alien	93,565	1.7%	—	181,493	2.6%	—	275,058	2.2%	—	34.0%
Total	5,508,223	100.0%	—	6,929,410	100.0%	—	12,437,633	100.0%	—	44.3%
1997										
Black	605,994	10.9%	36.4%	730,041	10.5%	42.5%	1,336,035	10.7%	39.5%	45.4%
Native American	71,258	1.3%	4.3%	54,652	0.8%	3.2%	125,910	1.0%	3.7%	56.6%
Asian/Pacific Islander	325,606	5.9%	19.6%	381,443	5.5%	22.2%	707,049	5.7%	20.9%	46.1%
Hispanic	661,542	11.9%	39.7%	551,723	7.9%	32.1%	1,213,265	9.7%	35.9%	54.5%
Minority subtotal	1,664,400	30.1%	100.0%	1,717,859	24.7%	100.0%	3,382,259	27.1%	100.0%	49.2%
White, non-Hispanic	3,581,854	64.7%	—	4,991,754	71.8%	—	8,573,608	68.7%	—	41.8%
Race/ethnicity unknown	210,241	3.8%	—	234,952	3.4%	—	445,193	3.6%	—	47.2%
Nonresident alien	81,483	1.5%	—	177,331	2.6%	—	258,814	2.1%	—	31.5%
Total	5,537,978	100.0%	—	6,950,883	100.0%	—	12,488,861	100.0%	—	44.3%
1998										
Black	619,093	11.2%	36.2%	763,870	10.7%	42.5%	1,382,963	10.9%	39.4%	44.8%
Native American	71,454	1.3%	4.2%	55,769	0.8%	3.1%	127,223	1.0%	3.6%	56.2%
Asian/Pacific Islander	344,356	6.2%	20.1%	393,400	5.5%	21.9%	737,756	5.8%	21.0%	46.7%
Hispanic	674,660	12.2%	39.5%	584,554	8.2%	32.5%	1,259,214	10.0%	35.9%	53.6%
Minority subtotal	1,709,563	30.9%	100.0%	1,797,593	25.3%	100.0%	3,507,156	27.7%	100.0%	48.7%
White, non-Hispanic	3,539,943	64.0%	—	4,857,116	68.3%	—	8,397,059	66.4%	—	42.2%
Race/ethnicity unknown	227,927	4.1%	—	274,104	3.9%	—	502,031	4.0%	—	45.4%
Nonresident alien	55,950	1.0%	—	185,144	2.6%	—	241,094	1.9%	—	23.2%
Total	5,533,383	100.0%	—	7,113,957	100.0%	—	12,647,340	100.0%	—	43.8%

Table 2.7 (cont'd)
Undergraduate Fall Enrollment by Race/Ethnicity: 1993–2002

	Community Colleges			4-Year Colleges			All Colleges			% enrolled in community colleges
		% of			% of			% of		
Race/Ethnicity	Fall enrollment	Total enrollment	Minority enrollment	Fall enrollment	Total enrollment	Minority enrollment	Fall enrollment	Total enrollment	Minority enrollment	
1999										
Black	630,611	11.3%	36.3%	777,420	10.8%	42.5%	1,408,031	11.0%	39.5%	44.8%
Native American	71,673	1.3%	4.1%	55,732	0.8%	3.0%	127,405	1.0%	3.6%	56.3%
Asian/Pacific Islander	337,294	6.1%	19.4%	401,219	5.6%	21.9%	738,513	5.8%	20.7%	45.7%
Hispanic	696,975	12.5%	40.1%	596,811	8.3%	32.6%	1,293,786	10.1%	36.3%	53.9%
Minority subtotal	1,736,553	31.2%	100.0%	1,831,182	25.5%	100.0%	3,567,735	28.0%	100.0%	48.7%
White, non-Hispanic	3,522,112	63.2%	—	4,861,312	67.6%	—	8,383,424	65.7%	—	42.0%
Race/ethnicity unknown	237,233	4.3%	—	303,987	4.2%	—	541,220	4.2%	—	43.8%
Nonresident alien	77,500	1.4%	—	189,591	2.6%	—	267,091	2.1%	—	29.0%
Total	5,573,398	100.0%	—	7,186,072	100.0%	—	12,759,470	100.0%	—	43.7%
2000										
Black	674,687	11.4%	35.1%	807,506	11.0%	42.2%	1,482,193	11.1%	38.7%	45.5%
Native American	74,175	1.2%	3.9%	57,154	0.8%	3.0%	131,329	1.0%	3.4%	56.5%
Asian/Pacific Islander	378,294	6.4%	19.7%	411,400	5.6%	21.5%	789,694	5.9%	20.6%	47.9%
Hispanic	792,755	13.3%	41.3%	635,592	8.6%	33.2%	1,428,347	10.7%	37.3%	55.5%
Minority subtotal	1,919,911	32.3%	100.0%	1,911,652	26.0%	100.0%	3,831,563	28.8%	100.0%	50.1%
White, non-Hispanic	3,633,929	61.2%	—	4,882,823	66.4%	—	8,516,752	64.0%	—	42.7%
Race/ethnicity unknown	298,319	5.0%	—	365,849	5.0%	—	664,168	5.0%	—	44.9%
Nonresident alien	90,212	1.5%	—	196,434	2.7%	—	286,646	2.2%	—	31.5%
Total	5,942,371	100.0%	—	7,356,758	100.0%	—	13,299,129	100.0%	—	44.7%
2001										
Black	724,646	11.6%	35.4%	854,422	11.2%	42.5%	1,579,068	11.4%	38.9%	45.9%
Native American	77,542	1.2%	3.8%	59,632	0.8%	3.0%	137,174	1.0%	3.4%	56.5%
Asian/Pacific Islander	394,643	6.3%	19.3%	428,766	5.6%	21.3%	823,409	5.9%	20.3%	47.9%
Hispanic	850,893	13.7%	41.6%	668,874	8.8%	33.2%	1,519,767	11.0%	37.4%	56.0%
Minority subtotal	2,047,724	32.9%	100.0%	2,011,694	26.3%	100.0%	4,059,418	29.3%	100.0%	50.4%
White, non-Hispanic	3,754,447	60.2%	—	4,990,959	65.4%	—	8,745,406	63.1%	—	42.9%
Race/ethnicity unknown	327,807	5.3%	—	428,038	5.6%	—	755,845	5.5%	—	43.4%
Nonresident alien	101,859	1.6%	—	203,865	2.7%	—	305,724	2.2%	—	33.3%
Total	6,231,837	100.0%	—	7,634,556	100.0%	—	13,866,393	100.0%	—	44.9%

| Race/Ethnicity | Community Colleges | | | 4-Year Colleges | | | All Colleges | | | % enrolled in community colleges |
| | Fall enrollment | % of | | Fall enrollment | % of | | Fall enrollment | % of | | |
		Total enrollment	Minority enrollment		Total enrollment	Minority enrollment		Total enrollment	Minority enrollment	
2002										
Black	785,627	12.0%	36.0%	886,885	11.3%	42.3%	1,672,512	11.6%	39.1%	47.0%
Native American	81,456	1.2%	3.7%	60,943	0.8%	2.9%	142,399	1.0%	3.3%	57.2%
Asian/Pacific Islander	415,354	6.3%	19.0%	444,072	5.7%	21.2%	859,426	6.0%	20.1%	48.3%
Hispanic	899,699	13.7%	41.2%	703,094	9.0%	33.6%	1,602,793	11.1%	37.5%	56.1%
Minority subtotal	2,182,136	33.3%	100.0%	2,094,994	26.7%	100.0%	4,277,130	29.7%	100.0%	51.0%
White, non-Hispanic	3,907,509	59.5%	—	5,058,633	64.4%	—	8,966,142	62.2%	—	43.6%
Race/ethnicity unknown	365,799	5.6%	—	492,466	6.3%	—	858,265	6.0%	—	42.6%
Nonresident alien	106,942	1.6%	—	207,595	2.6%	—	314,537	2.2%	—	34.0%
Total	6,562,386	100.0%	—	7,853,688	100.0%	—	14,416,074	100.0%	—	45.5%

Source: NCES (2004e)

Figure 2.4
Community College Enrollment by Race/Ethnicity: 1993

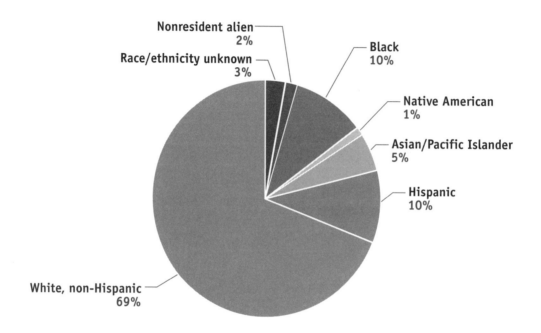

Nonresident alien
2%

Race/ethnicity unknown
3%

Black
10%

Native American
1%

Asian/Pacific Islander
5%

Hispanic
10%

White, non-Hispanic
69%

Source: NCES (2004e)

Figure 2.5

Community College Enrollment by Race/Ethnicity: 2002

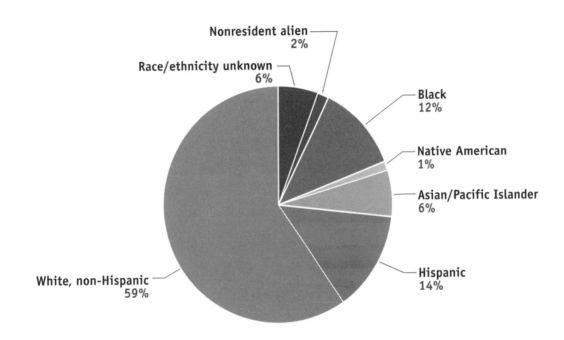

Source: NCES (2004e)

Table 2.8

Ethnic Origins of Hispanic Undergraduates: 1999–2000

College Type	Ethnic Origin				Total # of Hispanic students (estimated)
	Mexican, Mexican-American, or Chicano	Cuban	Puerto Rican	Other Hispanic origin	
Public community college	55.2%	2.3%	6.8%	30.0%	1,105,300
Public 4-year college	44.6%	4.4%	17.9%	28.7%	507,760
Independent nonprofit 4-year college	24.6%	3.6%	43.2%	23.8%	307,080
Proprietary college	44.3%	2.4%	18.9%	29.4%	294,700
More than one college	52.8%	4.6%	10.7%	26.9%	173,080
Total	47.6%	3.0%	15.7%	28.5%	2,426,340

Source: NCES (2005)

Note. Because of sampling methodology, some populations may be underrepresented.

Table 2.9

Ethnic Origins of Asian/Pacific Islander Undergraduates: 1999–2000

College Type	Ethnic Origin					
	Chinese	Korean	Filipino	Japanese	Vietnamese	Asian Indian
Public community college	23.5%	8.8%	12.7%	11.0%	16.7%	9.4%
Public 4-year college	27.4%	17.5%	6.3%	12.4%	10.6%	11.9%
Independent nonprofit 4-year college	28.0%	16.9%	11.8%	12.4%	3.5%	12.7%
Proprietary college	16.0%	9.7%	16.2%	9.5%	9.7%	9.0%
More than one college	25.6%	12.4%	10.8%	7.1%	18.8%	13.3%
Total	25.1%	13.1%	10.5%	11.2%	12.8%	11.0%

College Type	Ethnic Origin				Other Asian/ Pacific Islander	Total # of other Asian/Pacific Islanders (estimated)
	Thai	Native Hawaiian	Samoan	Guamanian or Chamorro		
Public community college	3.6%	—	—	—	14.4%	294,510
Public 4-year college	2.6%	0.8%	—	—	10.3%	262,230
Independent nonprofit 4-year college	2.0%	—	—	—	12.7%	86,870
Proprietary college	2.6%	—	—	—	27.3%	33,240
More than one college	1.8%	0.7%	—	—	9.6%	59,880
Total	2.9%	0.4%	—	—	13.1%	743,910

Source: NCES (2004j)

Note. Because of sampling methodology, some populations may be underrepresented.

Table 2.10

Immigrant Status of Undergraduates: 2003–2004

College Type	Immigrant Status			
	Resident alien/eligible noncitizen	Foreign-born citizen	Citizen, parents foreign born	All other citizens
Public community college	8.2%	6.1%	11.5%	74.2%
Public 4-year college	5.9%	5.2%	11.1%	77.9%
Independent nonprofit 4-year college	5.6%	6.5%	11.2%	76.7%
Proprietary college	8.2%	6.7%	13.9%	71.3%
More than one college	7.6%	6.2%	13.2%	73.1%
Total	7.1%	11.4%	17.6%	86.9%

Source: NCES (2005)

Table 2.11

Primary Language Spoken in the Home of Undergraduates: 1992–1993, 1995–1996, and 1999–2000

College Type	Primary Language Spoken							
	English	Spanish, Catalan, Galician, Basque	Chinese, Cantonese, Mandarin	Japanese	Korean	Arabic	German	Other
1992–1993								
Public community college	87.7%	5.3%	0.7%	0.2%	0.3%	0.4%	0.4%	5.0%
Public 4-year college	90.9%	3.5%	1.0%	0.2%	0.4%	0.3%	0.2%	3.6%
Independent nonprofit 4-year college	91.7%	4.4%	0.2%	0.4%	0.2%	0.2%	0.2%	2.7%
Proprietary college	82.7%	9.3%	0.6%	0.9%	0.3%	0.6%	0.2%	5.4%
More than one college	88.7%	3.9%	1.4%	0.3%	0.3%	0.4%	0.1%	5.0%
Total	88.6%	4.9%	0.8%	0.3%	0.4%	0.4%	0.3%	4.4%
1995–1996								
Public community college	87.5%	7.0%	0.5%	0.1%	0.1%	0.3%	0.4%	4.1%
Public 4-year college	90.3%	2.9%	1.2%	0.5%	0.4%	0.2%	0.1%	4.4%
Independent nonprofit 4-year college	88.8%	3.6%	0.9%	0.4%	1.2%	0.4%	0.1%	4.6%
Proprietary college	84.7%	9.7%	0.2%	0.1%	0.1%	0.1%	0.2%	4.9%
More than one college	85.2%	6.8%	1.2%	0.1%	0.6%	0.0%	0.1%	6.0%
Total	88.2%	5.4%	0.8%	0.3%	0.4%	0.2%	0.2%	4.5%
1999–2000								
Public community college	85.6%	6.2%	1.0%	0.4%	0.3%	0.3%	0.2%	6.0%
Public 4-year college	89.1%	4.5%	1.1%	0.4%	0.7%	0.2%	0.2%	3.9%
Independent nonprofit 4-year college	89.7%	4.4%	0.9%	0.1%	0.3%	0.2%	0.2%	4.2%
Proprietary college	83.5%	9.5%	0.8%	0.1%	0.2%	0.5%	0.1%	5.4%
More than one college	87.6%	4.7%	1.1%	0.3%	0.5%	0.3%	0.1%	5.5%
Total	87.3%	5.5%	1.0%	0.4%	0.4%	0.3%	0.2%	5.0%

Source: NCES (2004i, 2004j)

Note. Because of sampling methodology, some populations may be underrepresented.

Figure 2.6
Immigrant Status of Public Community College Students: 2003–2004

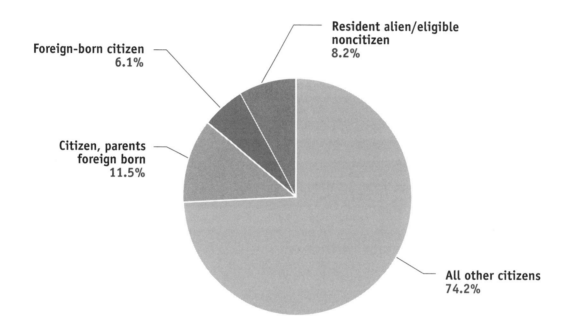

Resident alien/eligible noncitizen
8.2%

Foreign-born citizen
6.1%

Citizen, parents foreign born
11.5%

All other citizens
74.2%

Source: NCES (2005)

Table 2.12

Highest Level of Education Attained by Parents of Undergraduates: 1995–1996 and 1999–2000

College Type	Highest Level of Education Attained							
	Did not complete high school	High school diploma or equivalent	Less than 2 years of college	2 or more years of college/ AA degree	Bachelor's degree	Master's degree or equivalent	Doctoral/ professional degree	% first-generation student
1995–1996								
Public community college	11.2%	40.3%	10.0%	10.9%	17.7%	7.6%	2.5%	51.5%
Public 4-year college	4.5%	30.4%	7.8%	10.3%	25.3%	15.0%	6.7%	34.9%
Independent nonprofit 4-year college	5.1%	34.6%	5.8%	7.7%	21.7%	14.8%	10.4%	39.7%
Proprietary college	13.4%	50.6%	7.6%	8.9%	12.6%	5.0%	1.9%	64.0%
More than one college	8.8%	34.5%	6.7%	10.3%	19.7%	13.8%	6.2%	43.3%
Total	8.3%	36.8%	8.4%	10.1%	20.4%	11.1%	5.1%	45.1%
1999–2000								
Public community college	11.1%	34.2%	11.4%	12.6%	20.0%	7.6%	3.2%	45.3%
Public 4-year college	5.1%	24.0%	10.1%	12.3%	26.2%	15.6%	6.7%	29.1%
Independent nonprofit 4-year college	4.8%	23.6%	9.0%	10.2%	25.3%	16.2%	11.0%	28.4%
Proprietary college	11.5%	40.2%	10.5%	12.1%	16.3%	6.1%	3.2%	51.7%
More than one college	4.6%	24.9%	11.2%	14.6%	24.5%	14.2%	6.0%	29.5%
Total	7.9%	29.2%	10.6%	12.3%	22.8%	11.7%	5.6%	37.1%

Source: NCES (2004i, 2004j)

Note. Totals may not equal 100% because of rounding.

Table 2.13

Highest Level of Education Planned by Undergraduates: 1995–1996, 1999–2000, and 2003–2004

College Type	No degree or certificate	Certificate	Associate degree	Bachelor's degree	Post-baccalaureate certificate	Master's degree	Advanced degree: doctoral or first professional
1995–1996							
Public community college	3.0%	3.8%	12.0%	42.0%	0.4%	28.3%	10.5%
Public 4-year college	0.3%	0.3%	0.7%	19.9%	0.6%	54.4%	23.9%
Independent nonprofit 4-year college	0.5%	0.2%	0.7%	16.5%	0.4%	53.8%	27.9%
Proprietary college	2.4%	22.8%	14.5%	33.8%	0.2%	21.6%	4.7%
More than one college	0.3%	3.1%	3.9%	23.5%	0.7%	48.0%	20.4%
Total	1.6%	3.4%	6.6%	30.1%	0.5%	40.7%	17.3%
1999–2000							
Public community college	3.1%	3.6%	14.1%	42.9%	0.3%	28.7%	7.4%
Public 4-year college	0.5%	0.3%	1.3%	23.5%	0.4%	56.0%	18.1%
Independent nonprofit 4-year college	0.2%	0.2%	1.0%	19.9%	0.2%	56.7%	21.8%
Proprietary college	2.2%	11.6%	15.1%	40.6%	0.3%	24.8%	5.4%
More than one college	0.7%	1.1%	3.3%	25.0%	0.5%	52.0%	17.5%
Total	1.7%	2.4%	7.5%	32.3%	0.3%	42.5%	13.3%
2003–2004							
Public community college	1.1%	2.5%	15.1%	37.2%	0.5%	31.7%	12.0%
Public 4-year college	0.1%	0.2%	1.0%	23.9%	0.7%	50.2%	24.0%
Independent nonprofit 4-year college	0.1%	0.2%	0.9%	20.6%	0.7%	51.2%	26.4%
Proprietary college	1.3%	11.2%	12.2%	31.8%	0.6%	32.0%	10.9%
More than one college	0.5%	1.4%	5.2%	28.3%	0.9%	44.2%	19.6%
Total	0.6%	2.2%	8.0%	29.8%	0.6%	40.7%	18.0%

Source: NCES (2004i, 2004j, 2005)

Note. Totals may not equal 100% because of rounding.

Table 2.14

Highest Level of Education Planned by Public Community College Students, by Parents' Highest Level of Education Attained: 1999–2000

Highest Level of Education Planned by Students	Parents' Highest Level of Education Attained				
	Did not complete high school	High school diploma or equivalent	Vocational/ technical training	Less than 2 years of college	2 or more years of college/ AA degree
No degree or certificate	23.4%	39.9%	3.1%	3.7%	9.2%
Certificate	20.7%	45.8%	9.6%	3.8%	8.0%
Associate degree	14.3%	41.2%	2.4%	9.5%	13.0%
Bachelor's degree	10.2%	35.3%	3.4%	7.4%	12.8%
Master's degree	7.6%	27.5%	3.6%	8.0%	14.8%
Advanced degree: doctoral or first professional	9.4%	22.1%	2.5%	8.2%	11.0%
Total, all students	11.1%	34.2%	3.3%	8.1%	12.6%

Highest Level of Education Planned by Students	Parents' Highest Level of Education Attained			
	Bachelor's degree	Master's degree or equivalent	Professional degree	Doctoral degree or equivalent
No degree or certificate	11.7%	5.7%	0.9%	2.6%
Certificate	6.9%	3.6%	0.0%	1.6%
Associate degree	14.4%	3.9%	0.7%	0.7%
Bachelor's degree	23.3%	5.7%	1.0%	0.9%
Master's degree	22.2%	11.3%	2.9%	2.3%
Advanced degree: doctoral or first professional	22.7%	17.4%	3.0%	3.6%
Total, all students	20.0%	7.6%	1.6%	1.6%

Source: NCES (2004i, 2004j)

Note. Totals may not equal 100% because of rounding.

Table 2.15

Employment Status of Public Community College Students by Attendance Status and Age: 2003–2004

Age	Employment Status		
	Did not work	**Worked part time**	**Worked full time**
Attended full time, full year			
19 or younger	20.1%	64.5%	15.4%
20–22	18.3%	59.1%	22.6%
23–29	27.7%	40.6%	31.7%
30–39	30.5%	36.2%	33.4%
40 or older	36.7%	27.8%	35.5%
Total	23.1%	53.7%	23.3%
Attended part time, full year			
19 or younger	22.3%	53.5%	24.1%
20–22	14.2%	51.1%	34.7%
23–29	15.3%	33.4%	51.4%
30–39	20.4%	26.8%	52.9%
40 or older	21.6%	22.3%	56.1%
Total	18.5%	36.4%	45.1%
Attended full time, part year			
19 or younger	23.2%	54.8%	21.9%
20–22	18.9%	51.1%	30.0%
23–29	24.4%	35.5%	40.1%
30–39	38.3%	24.1%	37.6%
40 or older	37.5%	18.5%	44.0%
Total	25.4%	42.0%	32.7%
Attended part time, part year			
19 or younger	22.6%	46.3%	31.1%
20–22	16.3%	39.9%	43.9%
23–29	13.2%	29.8%	57.0%
30–39	19.3%	19.9%	60.8%
40 or older	18.8%	21.4%	59.8%
Total	17.5%	29.4%	53.2%
Total, all students			
19 or younger	21.6%	56.9%	21.5%
20–22	16.7%	50.1%	33.2%
23–29	17.6%	33.4%	49.0%
30–39	22.7%	25.0%	52.4%
40 or older	22.5%	22.1%	55.4%
Total	20.0%	38.4%	41.6%

Source: NCES (2005)

Note. Totals may not equal 100% because of rounding.

Table 2.16

Undergraduates' Self-Perceptions of Employment Status: 1995–1996, 1999–2000, and 2003–2004

College Type	Self-Perceptions of Status		
	Student who works	Employee who studies	Does not work
1995–1996			
Public community college	41.8%	41.9%	16.3%
Public 4-year college	59.6%	16.2%	24.2%
Independent nonprofit 4-year college	56.8%	21.0%	22.2%
Proprietary college	41.6%	31.7%	26.8%
More than one college	59.8%	19.3%	21.0%
Total	49.8%	29.0%	21.2%
1999–2000			
Public community college	37.7%	46.4%	15.9%
Public 4-year college	60.3%	16.6%	23.1%
Independent nonprofit 4-year college	54.3%	22.8%	22.9%
Proprietary college	45.1%	35.6%	19.3%
More than one college	55.1%	24.1%	20.8%
Total	48.4%	31.6%	20.0%
2003–2004			
Public community college	45.2%	34.9%	20.0%
Public 4-year college	61.6%	13.7%	24.7%
Independent nonprofit 4-year college	55.0%	21.1%	24.0%
Proprietary college	35.3%	41.5%	23.3%
More than one college	55.1%	24.0%	20.9%
Total	51.4%	26.3%	22.3%

Source: NCES (2004i, 2004j, 2005)

Figure 2.7

Employment Status of Public Community College Students by Attendance Status: 2003–2004

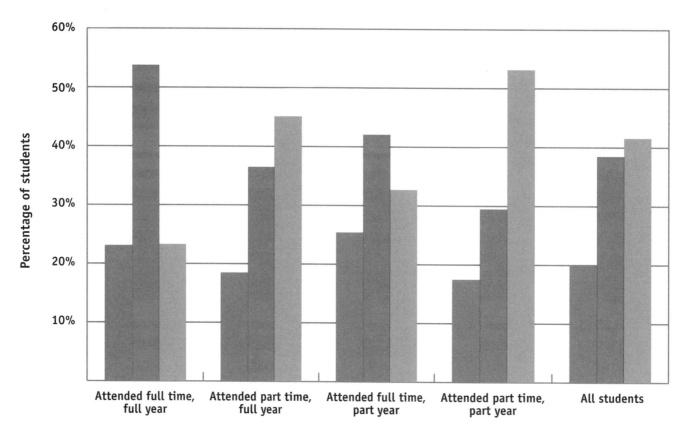

■ Did not work
■ Worked part time
■ Worked full time

Table 2.17

Percentage of Undergraduates With Risk Factors Associated With Decreased Persistence in College: 1995–1996, 1999–2000, and 2003–2004

College Type	Risk Factors								
	Independent student	Delayed enrollment	Enrolled less than full time	Has dependents	Single parent	Worked full time while enrolled	Has GED or no high school diploma	Has at least 1 risk factor	Average # of risk factors
1995–1996									
Public community college	62.4%	42.8%	71.0%	31.4%	14.8%	50.4%	11.0%	88.7%	2.4
Public 4-year college	37.0%	18.9%	32.9%	14.0%	5.7%	22.8%	3.0%	56.2%	1.2
Independent nonprofit 4-year college	42.2%	25.1%	31.0%	20.6%	7.4%	28.8%	4.7%	51.4%	1.4
Proprietary college	66.2%	48.2%	30.9%	38.5%	17.5%	38.7%	15.8%	84.2%	2.2
More than one college	45.9%	25.9%	41.4%	24.9%	11.6%	28.7%	7.3%	71.7%	1.7
Total	50.8%	32.1%	48.6%	24.5%	11.0%	36.4%	8.1%	72.7%	1.8
1999–2000									
Public community college	63.7%	58.7%	69.5%	34.5%	16.4%	52.6%	9.8%	90.7%	2.9
Public 4-year college	43.6%	39.3%	29.9%	23.3%	10.7%	32.4%	4.8%	60.6%	1.5
Independent nonprofit 4-year college	37.6%	31.5%	33.3%	17.6%	9.2%	24.7%	2.4%	60.8%	1.7
Proprietary college	69.1%	64.1%	25.8%	39.5%	21.6%	46.9%	10.7%	89.0%	2.6
More than one college	43.0%	34.0%	45.6%	23.1%	10.1%	33.7%	3.8%	73.8%	1.9
Total	50.9%	45.5%	47.9%	26.9%	13.3%	37.8%	6.5%	75.0%	2.2
2003–2004									
Public community college	61.2%	50.3%	66.1%	35.4%	17.2%	40.8%	11.6%	85.7%	2.4
Public 4-year college	34.3%	23.3%	30.2%	14.3%	6.3%	21.6%	3.6%	51.4%	1.1
Independent nonprofit 4-year college	37.7%	26.8%	26.7%	20.0%	9.0%	25.5%	4.5%	49.7%	1.3
Proprietary college	76.1%	57.2%	28.0%	46.2%	27.2%	47.6%	18.3%	88.9%	2.5
More than one college	48.1%	34.1%	44.9%	25.3%	11.6%	31.7%	6.9%	68.4%	1.7
Total	50.3%	38.4%	45.2%	27.1%	13.2%	32.7%	8.4%	69.5%	1.8

Source: NCES (2004i, 2004j, 2005)

Note. Risk factors are based on factors identified in NCES publications. See Horn (1996) for more detail.

Table 2.18

Income of Undergraduates by Dependency Status: 2003–2004

College Type	Income							% of students below $30,000	% of students below $50,000
	Less than $10,000	$10,000–$19,999	$20,000–$29,999	$30,000–$49,999	$50,000–$74,999	$75,000–$99,999	More than $100,000		
Dependent students (parents' income)									
Public community college	7.0%	8.6%	10.7%	21.4%	23.1%	12.9%	16.4%	26.2%	47.6%
Public 4-year college	4.3%	6.6%	8.3%	18.4%	22.9%	16.9%	22.6%	19.2%	37.6%
Independent nonprofit 4-year college	4.6%	6.4%	8.4%	17.2%	18.8%	17.6%	27.0%	19.4%	36.6%
Proprietary college	12.3%	14.1%	16.1%	21.1%	17.4%	9.2%	10.0%	42.4%	63.5%
More than one college	5.6%	7.1%	9.7%	18.6%	20.2%	15.9%	22.9%	22.4%	41.0%
Total	5.6%	7.5%	9.5%	19.3%	21.9%	15.4%	20.9%	22.6%	41.9%
Independent students (personal income)									
Public community college	20.6%	17.3%	15.6%	20.0%	14.7%	6.6%	5.3%	53.4%	73.4%
Public 4-year college	26.3%	19.2%	15.9%	17.5%	12.1%	5.0%	4.0%	61.4%	78.9%
Independent nonprofit 4-year college	20.9%	16.0%	15.6%	19.3%	15.6%	7.0%	5.6%	52.5%	71.8%
Proprietary college	25.5%	21.4%	17.4%	17.0%	11.4%	3.9%	3.4%	64.3%	81.3%
More than one college	21.7%	19.5%	14.4%	18.3%	15.4%	6.6%	4.2%	55.6%	73.9%
Total	22.5%	18.2%	15.8%	18.9%	13.9%	6.0%	4.7%	56.5%	75.4%
All students (parents' income for dependent students and personal income for independent students)									
Public community college	15.3%	13.9%	13.7%	20.6%	18.0%	9.0%	9.6%	42.9%	63.4%
Public 4-year college	11.8%	10.9%	10.9%	18.1%	19.2%	12.8%	16.2%	33.7%	51.8%
Independent nonprofit 4-year college	10.7%	10.0%	11.1%	18.0%	17.6%	13.6%	18.9%	31.9%	49.9%
Proprietary college	22.4%	19.7%	17.1%	17.9%	12.8%	5.2%	5.0%	59.1%	77.0%
More than one college	13.4%	13.1%	12.0%	18.4%	17.9%	11.4%	13.9%	38.4%	56.8%
Total	14.1%	12.9%	12.7%	19.1%	17.8%	10.7%	12.8%	39.7%	58.7%

Source: NCES (2005)

Note. Totals may not equal 100% because of rounding.

Table 2.19

Type of College Enrolled in by Full-Time, Full-Year Dependent Undergraduates by Family Income: 1989–1990 and 1999–2000

Family Income	College Type			
	Public community college	Public 4-year college	Independent nonprofit 4-year college	Proprietary less-than-4-year
1989–1990				
Lowest quarter	16.4%	47.0%	28.0%	8.7%
Lower middle quarter	19.7%	53.5%	22.8%	4.0%
Upper middle quarter	15.5%	56.4%	25.2%	2.9%
Highest quarter	10.6%	52.4%	35.7%	1.3%
Total	15.5%	52.4%	28.0%	4.1%
1999–2000				
Lowest quarter	24.7%	47.4%	22.9%	5.0%
Lower middle quarter	22.3%	51.9%	23.8%	2.0%
Upper middle quarter	18.6%	51.7%	28.0%	1.7%
Highest quarter	12.6%	53.9%	32.6%	0.9%
Total	19.4%	51.3%	27.0%	2.4%

Source: Choy (2004)

Note. Totals may not equal 100% because of rounding.

Table 2.20

Dependent Undergraduates' Income by Race/Ethnicity: 2003–2004

Race/Ethnicity	Income										% of students who are dependent
	Less than $10,000	$10,000–$19,999	$20,000–$29,999	$30,000–$39,999	$40,000–$49,999	$50,000–$59,999	$60,000–$69,999	$70,000–$79,999	$80,000–$99,999	$100,000 or more	
Public community colleges											
Black	14.1%	15.9%	17.7%	12.2%	10.5%	5.8%	5.7%	3.3%	5.9%	9.0%	28.9%
Native American	20.2%	6.8%	4.8%	16.5%	10.9%	8.7%	6.7%	2.0%	6.0%	17.6%	26.6%
Asian	12.5%	11.4%	12.2%	14.4%	8.5%	11.0%	6.5%	3.3%	8.7%	11.6%	41.9%
Hawaiian/other Pacific Islander	11.2%	6.5%	2.3%	9.6%	18.1%	7.0%	3.7%	—	9.0%	32.6%	52.8%
Hispanic	10.0%	13.4%	15.8%	10.9%	11.0%	9.0%	11.5%	2.9%	6.5%	9.2%	41.4%
White, non-Hispanic	4.2%	5.7%	8.1%	10.2%	10.6%	9.8%	10.8%	9.2%	11.6%	19.8%	40.3%
Other	8.1%	15.5%	14.8%	8.9%	6.6%	12.4%	6.8%	11.2%	2.0%	13.7%	43.6%
More than one race	6.6%	8.0%	11.8%	15.2%	7.6%	13.7%	6.7%	5.9%	8.8%	15.7%	39.9%
Total	7.0%	8.6%	10.7%	10.9%	10.5%	9.4%	9.8%	7.0%	9.7%	16.4%	38.8%
Public 4-year colleges											
Black	8.8%	14.2%	17.4%	11.4%	11.8%	6.6%	5.5%	6.4%	7.4%	10.6%	55.9%
Native American	4.2%	8.6%	6.3%	12.5%	13.5%	10.5%	10.6%	6.2%	14.6%	13.1%	51.3%
Asian	8.4%	11.5%	13.2%	9.2%	9.2%	6.3%	11.4%	5.7%	7.0%	18.0%	70.6%
Hawaiian/other Pacific Islander	8.9%	7.6%	1.4%	15.2%	1.9%	9.1%	17.4%	8.7%	9.1%	20.8%	70.4%
Hispanic	7.1%	16.5%	14.0%	10.9%	9.4%	10.0%	8.4%	4.6%	8.2%	10.9%	63.5%
White, non-Hispanic	3.0%	4.0%	6.1%	8.5%	9.2%	8.7%	10.8%	8.6%	15.0%	26.2%	67.2%
Other	4.1%	5.5%	12.1%	7.8%	7.1%	12.2%	15.2%	10.0%	10.8%	15.2%	59.0%
More than one race	3.1%	6.9%	9.8%	6.3%	10.4%	11.6%	11.7%	7.0%	14.5%	18.9%	68.2%
Total	4.3%	6.6%	8.3%	9.0%	9.5%	8.6%	10.3%	7.8%	13.2%	22.6%	65.7%
Independent nonprofit 4-year colleges											
Black	9.9%	12.6%	14.6%	13.5%	10.9%	7.8%	5.8%	8.1%	6.7%	10.2%	42.8%
Native American	—	—	—	—	—	—	—	—	—	—	40.7%
Asian	8.1%	8.1%	9.9%	10.8%	8.4%	8.2%	6.9%	6.3%	9.3%	24.0%	76.2%
Hawaiian/other Pacific Islander	—	—	—	—	—	—	—	—	—	—	—
Hispanic	12.6%	15.7%	14.2%	9.6%	9.7%	5.1%	7.0%	5.1%	7.1%	13.9%	55.7%
White, non-Hispanic	2.5%	4.2%	6.8%	7.6%	7.9%	7.6%	8.8%	7.7%	15.8%	31.1%	66.5%
Other	4.6%	6.1%	5.2%	17.2%	10.1%	10.0%	4.5%	3.3%	5.5%	33.5%	60.9%
More than one race	2.7%	5.8%	9.6%	13.6%	10.5%	5.0%	4.7%	5.5%	12.7%	30.0%	62.2%
Total	4.6%	6.4%	8.4%	8.7%	8.5%	7.4%	8.1%	7.4%	13.6%	27.0%	62.3%

	Income										% of students who are dependent
College Type	Less than $10,000	$10,000– $19,999	$20,000– $29,999	$30,000– $39,999	$40,000– $49,999	$50,000– $59,999	$60,000– $69,999	$70,000– $79,999	$80,000– $99,999	$100,000 or more	
Proprietary college											
Black	20.5%	17.2%	20.6%	15.1%	6.9%	6.0%	2.9%	3.9%	2.8%	4.1%	18.2%
Native American	—	—	—	—	—	—	—	—	—	—	16.1%
Asian	8.4%	15.1%	13.3%	12.4%	10.5%	5.8%	1.6%	8.2%	10.2%	14.6%	27.9%
Hawaiian/other Pacific Islander	—	—	—	—	—	—	—	—	—	—	28.9%
Hispanic	17.9%	19.6%	21.2%	11.1%	8.6%	6.6%	4.4%	3.8%	2.0%	4.9%	30.2%
White, non-Hispanic	6.5%	9.6%	12.3%	11.3%	10.4%	10.8%	9.2%	6.5%	9.8%	13.6%	23.8%
Other	22.2%	19.7%	9.3%	5.9%	6.3%	4.0%	5.7%	2.6%	3.6%	20.8%	22.4%
More than one race	8.1%	21.3%	14.7%	8.9%	7.2%	11.0%	6.4%	1.8%	7.7%	13.1%	24.0%
Total	12.3%	14.1%	16.1%	11.9%	9.2%	8.5%	6.4%	5.3%	6.4%	10.0%	23.9%
More than one college											
Black	12.6%	16.8%	18.8%	13.6%	6.1%	7.3%	3.9%	4.2%	8.4%	8.3%	39.3%
Native American	5.4%	1.4%	17.9%	8.5%	0.1%	0.0%	17.7%	9.2%	26.1%	13.7%	33.8%
Asian	10.1%	11.0%	13.0%	7.2%	9.6%	9.0%	6.4%	5.3%	10.5%	18.0%	63.9%
Hawaiian/other Pacific Islander	—	—	—	—	—	—	—	—	—	—	50.8%
Hispanic	7.6%	11.8%	15.4%	16.0%	12.2%	5.6%	8.4%	2.0%	8.1%	12.8%	48.9%
White, non-Hispanic	3.4%	4.4%	6.6%	8.9%	8.0%	7.3%	10.2%	8.1%	15.5%	27.7%	53.9%
Other	6.5%	8.0%	15.8%	19.3%	7.7%	5.6%	8.4%	2.8%	7.7%	18.2%	56.4%
More than one race	8.2%	2.8%	7.6%	7.7%	15.3%	7.8%	5.4%	12.9%	4.1%	28.4%	47.6%
Total	5.6%	7.1%	9.7%	10.1%	8.5%	7.3%	9.0%	6.7%	13.1%	22.9%	51.9%
Total, all college types											
Black	12.0%	14.9%	17.4%	12.4%	10.4%	6.5%	5.4%	5.2%	6.5%	9.4%	36.0%
Native American	9.6%	7.2%	7.7%	13.3%	10.9%	8.9%	10.3%	5.2%	13.0%	13.8%	35.0%
Asian	9.8%	11.0%	12.5%	10.8%	9.0%	8.3%	8.4%	5.1%	8.4%	16.8%	56.4%
Hawaiian/other Pacific Islander	8.6%	6.8%	3.4%	11.4%	10.4%	9.1%	9.1%	5.0%	8.5%	27.9%	55.7%
Hispanic	10.1%	15.0%	15.5%	11.2%	10.2%	8.3%	9.1%	3.7%	6.8%	10.3%	46.8%
White, non-Hispanic	3.4%	4.7%	7.0%	8.9%	9.3%	8.8%	10.4%	8.5%	14.0%	25.0%	53.0%
Other	6.7%	10.0%	12.3%	10.7%	7.4%	10.9%	9.4%	8.3%	6.3%	18.0%	48.9%
More than one race	4.8%	7.4%	10.5%	10.5%	9.6%	11.0%	8.3%	6.7%	11.4%	19.9%	50.2%
Total	5.6%	7.5%	9.5%	9.8%	9.5%	8.5%	9.5%	7.3%	11.9%	20.9%	49.7%

Source: NCES (2005)

Table 2.21

Independent Undergraduates' Income by Race/Ethnicity: 2003–2004

Race/Ethnicity	Income						% of students who are independent
	Less than $5,000	$5,000–$9,999	$10,000–$19,999	$20,000–$29,999	$30,000–$49,999	$50,000 or more	
Public community college							
Black	16.2%	11.0%	23.6%	18.3%	17.8%	13.1%	71.1%
Native American	14.0%	7.4%	18.7%	13.6%	22.3%	24.1%	73.4%
Asian	16.6%	6.4%	14.9%	10.2%	21.2%	30.7%	58.1%
Hawaiian/other Pacific Islander	17.8%	3.7%	17.7%	6.9%	24.9%	29.2%	47.2%
Hispanic	13.7%	8.9%	20.1%	17.3%	18.3%	21.8%	58.6%
White, non-Hispanic	9.7%	8.0%	14.8%	15.0%	20.7%	31.8%	59.7%
Other	15.9%	18.2%	18.0%	11.7%	17.2%	19.1%	56.4%
More than one race	7.9%	9.0%	19.5%	14.6%	26.5%	22.6%	60.2%
Total	11.9%	8.7%	17.3%	15.6%	20.0%	26.6%	61.2%
Public 4-year college							
Black	16.9%	12.7%	20.4%	17.9%	15.4%	16.7%	44.1%
Native American	6.7%	14.9%	25.5%	14.4%	17.3%	21.2%	48.8%
Asian	29.0%	14.6%	12.8%	9.2%	14.2%	20.3%	29.4%
Hawaiian/other Pacific Islander	—	—	—	—	—	—	29.7%
Hispanic	12.8%	13.0%	22.1%	20.1%	17.9%	14.1%	36.5%
White, non-Hispanic	13.4%	10.9%	19.1%	15.4%	18.1%	23.2%	32.8%
Other	15.5%	17.3%	8.8%	19.6%	22.0%	16.8%	41.0%
More than one race	13.2%	14.6%	17.3%	15.8%	17.7%	21.4%	31.8%
Total	14.6%	11.8%	19.2%	15.9%	17.5%	21.1%	34.3%
Independent nonprofit 4-year college							
Black	13.0%	10.5%	17.5%	22.4%	18.6%	18.1%	57.2%
Native American	—	—	—	—	—	—	59.3%
Asian	21.7%	10.5%	22.1%	8.4%	20.6%	16.8%	23.8%
Hawaiian/other Pacific Islander	—	—	—	—	—	—	—
Hispanic	18.6%	10.8%	18.3%	15.1%	19.6%	17.6%	44.3%
White, non-Hispanic	9.7%	7.6%	14.9%	13.7%	19.3%	34.8%	33.6%
Other	10.9%	17.7%	18.1%	16.2%	9.9%	27.3%	39.1%
More than one race	14.3%	8.9%	5.9%	19.8%	22.6%	28.5%	37.8%
Total	12.0%	8.9%	16.0%	15.6%	19.3%	28.2%	37.7%

Race/Ethnicity	Income						% of students who are independent
	Less than $5,000	$5,000-$9,999	$10,000-$19,999	$20,000-$29,999	$30,000-$49,999	$50,000 or more	
Proprietary college							
Black	15.6%	12.5%	23.7%	22.0%	13.3%	13.0%	81.8%
Native American	10.1%	13.4%	11.7%	31.9%	15.4%	17.6%	83.9%
Asian	17.1%	10.4%	23.3%	11.0%	11.9%	26.4%	72.1%
Hawaiian/other Pacific Islander	10.0%	5.3%	10.7%	33.7%	27.1%	13.2%	71.1%
Hispanic	15.1%	15.1%	25.0%	16.6%	15.4%	12.8%	69.8%
White, non-Hispanic	12.4%	9.6%	18.2%	15.7%	20.0%	24.1%	76.2%
Other	13.4%	22.3%	31.8%	8.0%	12.5%	12.1%	77.6%
More than one race	13.8%	10.2%	30.2%	18.4%	15.7%	11.8%	76.0%
Total	13.9%	11.6%	21.4%	17.4%	17.0%	18.7%	76.1%
More than one college							
Black	14.3%	13.0%	20.6%	20.5%	16.9%	14.8%	60.7%
Native American	27.7%	9.0%	14.7%	19.9%	5.8%	22.9%	66.2%
Asian	26.4%	6.3%	13.0%	10.6%	19.2%	24.4%	36.1%
Hawaiian/other Pacific Islander	—	—	—	—	—	—	49.2%
Hispanic	11.1%	10.9%	23.7%	14.6%	17.9%	21.8%	51.1%
White, non-Hispanic	9.9%	7.9%	19.1%	13.3%	19.2%	30.6%	46.1%
Other	22.7%	12.1%	20.6%	5.5%	11.0%	28.2%	43.6%
More than one race	20.2%	10.6%	17.9%	8.4%	19.6%	23.4%	52.4%
Total	12.6%	9.1%	19.5%	14.4%	18.3%	26.1%	48.1%
Total, all colleges							
Black	15.8%	11.6%	22.2%	19.5%	16.6%	14.3%	64.0%
Native American	13.5%	10.5%	19.2%	16.4%	19.1%	21.4%	65.0%
Asian	20.8%	8.8%	15.4%	9.9%	18.6%	26.5%	43.6%
Hawaiian/other Pacific Islander	19.6%	4.7%	20.3%	13.2%	19.9%	22.3%	44.4%
Hispanic	14.2%	10.9%	21.3%	17.2%	17.8%	18.7%	53.2%
White, non-Hispanic	10.9%	8.8%	16.5%	14.9%	19.8%	29.2%	47.0%
Other	15.5%	18.0%	18.4%	12.8%	16.4%	18.9%	51.1%
More than one race	11.3%	10.4%	19.0%	15.3%	22.6%	21.5%	49.8%
Total	12.8%	9.7%	18.2%	15.8%	18.9%	24.6%	50.3%

Source: NCES (2005)

Table 2.22

Percentage of Undergraduates Who Attended College In-State and Distance From Home: 1999–2000

College Type	% attended in-state	Distance From Home, All Students		
		Average miles	Median miles	90th percentile in miles from home
Public community college	95.5%	33	9	40
Public 4-year college	88.8%	100	22	235
Independent nonprofit 4-year college	65.2%	214	31	781
Proprietary college	87.3%	81	14	182
More than one college	86.3%	93	14	206
Total	88.2%	86	13	191

Source: NCES (2004j)

Figure 2.8
Distribution of Main Limiting Condition for Undergraduates With Disabilities: 1999–2000

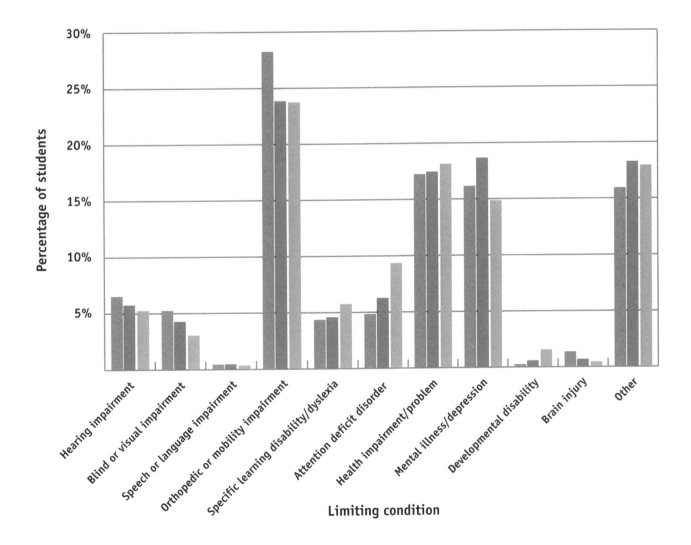

- ■ Public community college
- ■ Public 4-year college
- ■ Independent nonprofit 4-year college

III

The Social and Economic Impact of Community Colleges

Just as investors do in the business world, those who use community college services demand a high return on investment (ROI). Community college students want assurance that their academic efforts and tuition dollars will result in real learning for their many life roles, as well as increased earnings. Employers want well-prepared workers who can be productive in a highly competitive global workplace. Community colleges want to be sure that they are fulfilling their missions and making substantial contributions to the quality of life of the residents in their communities. And legislators want to know that public funds are being used efficiently to help people become contributing members of society.

Individual students can count on a high ROI for their tuition dollars. According to the 2002 census, full-time year-round workers between the ages of 25 and 64 with high school diplomas earned an average of $34,547 annually, whereas workers with associate degrees

earned an average of $42,204 each year (U.S. Census Bureau, 2004a). These earnings compound over the course of a worker's lifetime. High school dropouts might expect to earn $1 million (1999 dollars) if they are employed steadily over 40 years of work life, and high school graduates might expect to earn $1.2 million. Those with an associate degree can earn $1.6 million, and those with a baccalaureate—which many community college students eventually achieve—can earn $2.1 million during their work lives. Clearly, education pays off.

Unfortunately, these data also show that women and minorities still earn less than men and Whites for comparable work. However, their earnings are higher when they have a college degree, and the incremental value of these degrees is as high or even higher than it is for Whites. For many thousands of women and minority students, community colleges are the entry point to higher levels of education and higher earnings over a lifetime.

A study conducted recently of the 39 community college districts in Illinois shows that a college education can provide significant financial benefits for students (Illinois Community College Board, 2002). This study revealed that the average annual earnings of a person with an associate degree were 112.6% more than those of someone who did not complete high school and 34% more than those of someone with a high school diploma or GED. Over a work life of 35 to 40 years, associate degree holders may earn as much as $350,000 more than their less-educated colleagues. Moreover, students in Illinois had a 26.1% return on their education investments and recovered all costs in 5.6 years. These findings show that a student's standard of living is likely to increase and the community is likely to benefit economically through consumer spending and increased tax revenues.

In addition to increasing one's earning potential, a college education increases a person's work options, according to the Employment Policy Foundation (EPF). EPF tracks job gains and losses in different industry sectors and reported in late 2001 that manufacturing job losses continued throughout that year while job gains occurred in the retail sector, education services, medical services, construction, and finance—fields all requiring higher skill levels.

Furthermore, when filling vacant positions, employers sought specific higher-order skills and preferred graduates who had completed systematic programs of study. The job applicant's possession of a college degree was seen as a valuable job asset. Concluding that the American job market was experiencing a profound structural change, EPF advised those who want to take advantage of the new economy to complete a college degree and seek work in growth career fields. Students in community colleges are doing just that.

Of course, the impact of community college education extends beyond economic capacity. A "Faces of the Future" survey conducted by AACC indicated that students value the intellectual growth and increased self-confidence resulting from their time in college (VanDerLinden, 2002). When asked to rate their colleges, the majority of students reported that they were satisfied or

very satisfied with the learning environment and campus climate and with the respect they received from instructors and staff. For these students, then, community college studies offer an opportunity for personal growth and the development of broader perspectives that can be applied in their family and civic lives as well as at work. Very often, their academic success inspires students to undertake further study toward a baccalaureate, a goal they might not have contemplated before, an undertaking that expands their economic and personal options even more.

Community colleges are addressing the demand for ROI with increasingly sophisticated economic models that calculate the benefits of investing taxpayer dollars in these colleges. Research indicates that every dollar invested in a community college yields an average of $3.00 in benefits back to the taxpayers (ACCT, 2003). These benefits include the increased capacity of students as wage earners and taxpayers and reduced costs for public services such as incarceration and health care.

For example, the study conducted by the Illinois community college districts addressed the role those colleges played in the state economy. In 2001, the combined budget of these districts was $1.9 billion, and $1.2 billion (63%) was spent in the form

of wages, salaries, and supply purchases that flowed directly into the Illinois economy. Skills acquired by workers through coursework at community colleges increased by $10.1 billion the output of the Illinois industries in which these workers were employed. Moreover, because community college students tend to stay in the local area, they constitute a long-term economic resource for the state. Further calculations revealed that taxpayers' support for Illinois community colleges in 2001 ($1.1 billion) would be fully recovered in 9.1 years in the form of higher tax revenues and reduced public expenditures for unemployment, welfare, and other services.

Similarly, an economic impact study of the Virginia Community College System (VCCS) in 2000–2001 showed that the estimated dollar value of increased workforce productivity as a result of coursework at these colleges was approximately $395 million per year (Virginia Community College System, 2003). The value of the future stream of benefits from that productivity increase was close to $3.7 billion. The findings indicated that for every tax dollar invested in the community colleges, $2.20 accrued to Virginia's economy. Noting that the VCCS enrolled 63% of undergraduates in the state, the findings also suggested that

Virginia would need nearly $400 million in additional tax dollars to accommodate these students at four-year colleges.

Yet another study by the Los Angeles Community Colleges District showed comparable results (Los Angeles Community Colleges, 2002). Taking into account the economic activity generated by district expenditures ($964 million in wages, salaries, benefits, supplies, and operating expenses), the economic activity generated by students' expenditures ($354 million spent by more than 100,000 full-time equivalent students) and the greater annual income of former students ($5.3 billion), the Los Angeles colleges estimated that they pumped $6.6 billion into the local economy in 2000–2001. Based on such studies, legislators and business leaders can be assured that community colleges are major forces in state economies and provide a very real ROI for their communities.

Community colleges contribute to the economy in another important way—they offer programs in career fields where there is the most demand both locally and nationally. Each year, AACC identifies hot programs—courses of study from which students are hired immediately upon graduation, and sometimes even before they complete their degrees. According to the most recent survey

(McPhee, 2004), 46% of the hot programs identified by the responding colleges (for-credit and noncredit) were in allied health fields. The five hottest programs were registered nursing, law enforcement, licensed practical nursing, radiology, and computer technologies. Registered nursing was the hottest program in all six regions of the country, and LPN, radiology, and law enforcement were hot in three or more regions. Entry-level jobs in these fields generally paid higher starting salaries, ranging from $27,500 to $38,400 per year, although the salaries varied depending on the region. These findings were similar to the Bureau of Labor Statistics's predictions that between 2002 and 2012, 6 of the top 10 growth occupations will be in allied health fields, which are expected to grow by 32% (Hecker, 2004). Similarly, during the height of the technology boom, computer technologies courses and programs were the most frequently added by colleges. Additionally, graduates of those programs received some of the highest starting salaries reported (McPhee, 2004).

Community colleges will continue to be the primary providers of education for these workers, through either degrees and certificates or noncredit training programs. For that reason, they are continually adjusting their curricula to meet

local employment needs. Twenty-six percent of the respondents to the 2004 hot programs survey noted that in the past three years they had added courses or programs in allied health fields; 17% added offerings in information technologies, and 14.7% added offerings in the skilled trades—industrial field. These additions included programs with both for-credit and noncredit courses. Also, of the 65.4% of respondents who noted that they had revised their curricula to address homeland security needs, half indicated that they had added courses or entire programs in a related area. Emerging career areas associated with homeland security include first responders, security and protective services, infrastructure security, and cybersecurity.

Given the benefits of degrees for individuals and society, the less-than-optimal college participation rates found in many states today is a continuing concern. The American workforce must be prepared to compete in today's global economy, yet—according to a 2003 report of the Education Commission of the States—rates of high school completion are somewhat stagnant, and young people who do complete high school may find it impossible to enroll because financing a college education is beyond their means. Women, minorities, new immigrants, and other nontraditional populations may not be participating in postsecondary education at desirable rates either. Community colleges will need to continue their commitment to providing access in order to reduce the current participation gap and ensure that our nation is positioned for economic strength with a highly educated workforce.

All in all, legislators, business leaders, the general public, and students themselves can count on community colleges to provide a real ROI as they carry out their missions. As was noted in *The Knowledge Net: Connecting Communities, Learners, and Colleges*—the report of the AACC New Expeditions futuring project conducted in 2000 with funding from the W. K. Kellogg Foundation—community colleges are the nexus of a constantly changing world. They connect with local communities through education and enrichment programs and contribute substantially to the economy and to the quality of life. They link the various levels of the American education system and draw students to learning-centered campuses for a lifetime of growth and development. The impact of community colleges has been felt for the past 100 years, and they are poised to play an even more central role in the learning network of our country in the next century. ⊕

Table 3.1

Highest Level of Education Attained by People Aged 25 or Older: 1993–2002 (numbers in thousands)

Highest Level of Education Attained	1993	1994	1995	1996	1997	1998	1999	2000	2001	2002	% change 1993–2002
# of people aged 25 or older											
None	1,010	1,012	1,005	966	916	844	848	851	892	870	-13.9%
Elementary grades 1–4	2,370	2,144	2,069	2,061	1,924	1,990	1,894	1,891	1,918	2,032	-14.3%
Elementary grades 5–6	3,484	3,622	3,620	3,479	3,548	3,614	3,621	3,542	3,633	3,789	8.8%
Elementary grades 7–8	8,263	7,737	7,253	7,116	6,929	6,334	6,034	5,896	5,886	5,880	-28.8%
High school grade 9	3,967	3,986	3,965	4,133	4,026	3,902	3,657	3,680	3,859	3,751	-5.4%
High school grade 10	5,724	5,860	5,667	5,808	5,605	5,297	5,332	4,975	5,014	5,037	-12.0%
High school grade 11	7,376	7,079	6,934	7,161	7,580	7,577	7,454	7,019	7,406	7,589	2.9%
High school diploma	57,589	56,515	56,450	56,559	57,586	58,714	57,935	58,086	58,272	58,456	1.5%
Some college, no degree	27,095	28,554	29,355	29,201	29,367	29,638	30,102	30,753	31,441	30,991	14.4%
Associate degree	10,356	11,460	11,894	12,171	12,407	12,868	13,074	13,692	14,840	15,051	45.3%
Occupational associate degree	5,962	6,327	6,384	6,495	6,527	6,767	6,884	7,221	7,849	8,070	35.4%
Academic associate degree	4,394	5,133	5,510	5,676	5,880	6,101	6,190	6,471	6,991	6,981	58.9%
Bachelor's degree	23,619	24,256	25,313	26,540	27,357	28,305	29,495	29,840	31,500	32,282	36.7%
Master's degree	8,310	8,398	8,817	9,101	9,132	9,232	9,767	10,396	10,978	11,487	38.2%
Professional degree	2,236	2,267	2,428	2,416	2,447	2,568	2,502	2,586	2,605	2,737	22.4%
Doctorate	1,425	1,623	1,668	1,611	1,761	1,868	2,039	2,023	2,145	2,190	53.7%
Total	162,826	164,512	166,438	168,323	170,581	172,751	173,754	175,230	180,389	182,142	11.9%

Highest Level of Education Attained	Year										% change 1993–2002
	1993	1994	1995	1996	1997	1998	1999	2000	2001	2002	
% of people aged 25 or older											
None	0.6%	0.6%	0.6%	0.6%	0.5%	0.5%	0.5%	0.5%	0.5%	0.5%	-23.0%
Elementary grades 1–4	1.5%	1.3%	1.2%	1.2%	1.1%	1.2%	1.1%	1.1%	1.1%	1.1%	-23.4%
Elementary grades 5–6	2.1%	2.2%	2.2%	2.1%	2.1%	2.1%	2.1%	2.0%	2.0%	2.1%	-2.8%
Elementary grades 7–8	5.1%	4.7%	4.4%	4.2%	4.1%	3.7%	3.5%	3.4%	3.3%	3.2%	-36.4%
High school grade 9	2.4%	2.4%	2.4%	2.5%	2.4%	2.3%	2.1%	2.1%	2.1%	2.1%	-15.5%
High school grade 10	3.5%	3.6%	3.4%	3.5%	3.3%	3.1%	3.1%	2.8%	2.8%	2.8%	-21.3%
High school grade 11	4.5%	4.3%	4.2%	4.3%	4.4%	4.4%	4.3%	4.0%	4.1%	4.2%	-8.0%
High school diploma	35.4%	34.4%	33.9%	33.6%	33.8%	34.0%	33.3%	33.1%	32.3%	32.1%	-9.3%
Some college, no degree	16.6%	17.4%	17.6%	17.3%	17.2%	17.2%	17.3%	17.6%	17.4%	17.0%	2.2%
Associate degree	6.4%	7.0%	7.1%	7.2%	7.3%	7.4%	7.5%	7.8%	8.2%	8.3%	29.9%
Occupational associate degree	3.7%	3.8%	3.8%	3.9%	3.8%	3.9%	4.0%	4.1%	4.4%	4.4%	21.0%
Academic associate degree	2.7%	3.1%	3.3%	3.4%	3.4%	3.5%	3.6%	3.7%	3.9%	3.8%	42.0%
Bachelor's degree	14.5%	14.7%	15.2%	15.8%	16.0%	16.4%	17.0%	17.0%	17.5%	17.7%	22.2%
Master's degree	5.1%	5.1%	5.3%	5.4%	5.4%	5.3%	5.6%	5.9%	6.1%	6.3%	23.6%
Professional degree	1.4%	1.4%	1.5%	1.4%	1.4%	1.5%	1.4%	1.5%	1.4%	1.5%	9.4%
Doctorate	0.9%	1.0%	1.0%	1.0%	1.0%	1.1%	1.2%	1.2%	1.2%	1.2%	37.4%
Total	100.0%	100.0%	100.0%	100.0%	100.0%	100.0%	100.0%	100.0%	100.0%	100.0%	

Source: U.S. Census Bureau (1998, 1999, 2000, 2001, 2002, 2003, 2004a)

Note. Details may not equal totals because of rounding. High school diploma includes GED or high school equivalency.

Table 3.2

Highest Level of Education Attained by People Aged 25 or Older, by Gender and Race/Ethnicity: 2002

Highest Level of Education Attained	Men # (1,000s)	Men %	Women # (1,000s)	Women %	Total # (1,000s)	Total %
White, non-Hispanic						
No high school	798	1.2%	745	1.1%	1,543	1.2%
Some high school, no diploma	6,599	10.3%	6,939	10.0%	13,538	10.1%
High school diploma	20,197	31.5%	23,801	34.3%	43,998	33.0%
Associate degree	5,095	8.0%	6,639	9.6%	11,734	8.8%
Occupational associate degree	2,867	4.5%	3,503	5.1%	6,370	4.8%
Academic associate degree	2,228	3.5%	3,136	4.5%	5,364	4.0%
Some college, no degree	11,068	17.3%	12,309	17.8%	23,377	17.5%
Bachelor's degree	12,936	20.2%	12,841	18.5%	25,777	19.3%
Master's degree	4,626	7.2%	4,819	7.0%	9,445	7.1%
Professional degree	1,524	2.4%	713	1.0%	2,237	1.7%
Doctorate	1,240	1.9%	526	0.8%	1,766	1.3%
Total	64,083	100.0%	69,332	100.0%	133,415	100.0%
Black, non-Hispanic						
No high school	333	3.9%	323	2.9%	656	3.3%
Some high school, no diploma	1,473	17.1%	1,955	17.7%	3,428	17.5%
High school diploma	2,995	34.9%	3,671	33.2%	6,666	33.9%
Some college, no degree	1,784	20.8%	2,141	19.4%	3,925	20.0%
Associate degree	589	6.9%	1,005	9.1%	1,594	8.1%
Occupational associate degree	301	3.5%	510	4.6%	811	4.1%
Academic associate degree	288	3.4%	495	4.5%	783	4.0%
Bachelor's degree	996	11.6%	1,340	12.1%	2,336	11.9%
Master's degree	293	3.4%	496	4.5%	789	4.0%
Professional degree	66	0.8%	76	0.7%	142	0.7%
Doctorate	63	0.7%	42	0.4%	105	0.5%
Total	8,592	100.0%	11,049	100.0%	19,641	100.0%

Source: U.S. Census Bureau (2004a)

Note. Too few Native Americans were included in the sample to produce reliable estimates. High school diploma includes GED or equivalency.

Highest Level of Education Attained	Men # (1,000s)	Men %	Women # (1,000s)	Women %	Total # (1,000s)	Total %
Asian/Pacific Islander						
No high school	108	2.9%	283	6.9%	391	5.0%
Some high school, no diploma	284	7.6%	312	7.6%	596	7.6%
High school diploma	769	20.6%	957	23.2%	1,726	21.9%
Some college, no degree	438	11.7%	455	11.0%	893	11.4%
Associate degree	239	6.4%	309	7.5%	548	7.0%
Occupational associate degree	114	3.0%	156	3.8%	270	3.4%
Academic associate degree	125	3.3%	153	3.7%	278	3.5%
Bachelor's degree	1,148	30.7%	1,289	31.3%	2,437	31.0%
Master's degree	470	12.6%	355	8.6%	825	10.5%
Professional degree	127	3.4%	86	2.1%	213	2.7%
Doctorate	158	4.2%	78	1.9%	236	3.0%
Total	3,741	100.0%	4,124	100.0%	7,865	100.0%
Hispanic						
No high school	2,113	21.3%	1,960	20.1%	4,073	20.7%
Some high school, no diploma	2,245	22.6%	2,147	22.0%	4,392	22.3%
High school diploma	2,727	27.5%	2,766	28.4%	5,493	27.9%
Some college, no degree	1,252	12.6%	1,239	12.7%	2,491	12.7%
Associate degree	491	5.0%	550	5.6%	1,041	5.3%
Occupational associate degree	267	2.7%	277	2.8%	544	2.8%
Academic associate degree	224	2.3%	273	2.8%	497	2.5%
Bachelor's degree	781	7.9%	811	8.3%	1,592	8.1%
Master's degree	184	1.9%	197	2.0%	381	1.9%
Professional degree	76	0.8%	65	0.7%	141	0.7%
Doctorate	47	0.5%	21	0.2%	68	0.3%
Total	9,916	100.0%	9,756	100.0%	19,672	100.0%
All people aged 25 or older						
No high school	3,360	3.9%	3,331	3.5%	6,691	3.7%
Some high school, no diploma	10,735	12.3%	11,523	12.1%	22,258	12.2%
High school diploma	26,947	31.0%	31,509	33.1%	58,456	32.1%
Some college, no degree	14,661	16.9%	16,330	17.2%	30,991	17.0%
Associate degree	6,466	7.4%	8,585	9.0%	15,051	8.3%
Occupational associate degree	3,577	4.1%	4,493	4.7%	8,070	4.4%
Academic associate degree	2,889	3.3%	4,092	4.3%	6,981	3.8%
Bachelor's degree	15,925	18.3%	16,357	17.2%	32,282	17.7%
Master's degree	5,595	6.4%	5,893	6.2%	11,488	6.3%
Professional degree	1,795	2.1%	942	1.0%	2,737	1.5%
Doctorate	1,514	1.7%	676	0.7%	2,190	1.2%
Total	86,998	100.0%	95,146	100.0%	182,144	100.0%

Table 3.3

Mean and Median Earnings of Workers Aged 25 or Older, by Education, Race/Ethnicity, and Gender: 2002

Race/Ethnicity and Gender	High School Education			College Education			Bachelor's degree or higher			
	Some high school, no diploma	High school diploma	Some college, no degree	Associate degree	Bachelor's degree	Master's degree	Professional degree	Doctorate	Bachelor's or higher	All workers
Mean earnings										
All employees										
Hispanic	$20,035	$26,078	$31,163	$33,250	$42,254	$59,064	$81,186	—	$49,417	$28,165
White, non-Hispanic	$23,456	$30,597	$37,129	$36,553	$55,236	$61,132	$117,862	$91,773	$61,982	$42,943
Black	$18,089	$24,662	$30,348	$31,266	$43,394	$52,348	$98,286	$69,780	$48,199	$30,783
Asian/Pacific Islander	$18,191	$25,942	$33,149	$32,679	$47,935	$64,581	$98,894	$80,884	$57,794	$44,021
Men	$24,591	$35,144	$42,016	$44,655	$65,482	$79,217	$120,436	$95,928	$74,334	$48,268
Women	$16,120	$21,747	$26,694	$28,324	$38,045	$48,123	$63,717	$62,200	$42,401	$29,296
Total	$21,204	$29,185	$35,370	$35,590	$53,103	$60,726	$113,242	$89,638	$60,027	$39,849
Year-round, full-time employees										
Hispanic	$23,840	$30,124	$36,320	$39,577	$48,692	$64,215	$96,055	—	$56,527	$33,199
White, non-Hispanic	$29,805	$36,440	$44,244	$43,487	$65,082	$70,709	$131,983	$103,325	$72,455	$51,436
Black	$22,813	$29,140	$35,349	$36,395	$48,105	$57,716	$104,997	—	$53,362	$36,232
Asian/Pacific Islander	$21,313	$30,070	$39,786	$38,256	$56,016	$71,773	$102,507	$86,300	$65,529	$50,838
Men	$28,512	$39,017	$46,696	$48,153	$71,361	$87,099	$130,764	$104,237	$81,130	$53,917
Women	$21,835	$27,525	$33,002	$34,560	$45,778	$57,874	$72,689	$70,302	$50,772	$36,384
Total	$25,988	$34,547	$41,961	$42,204	$61,994	$69,625	$126,028	$99,764	$69,534	$47,454

	High School Education		College Education						Bachelor's degree or higher	
Race/Ethnicity and Gender	**Some high school, no diploma**	**High school diploma**	**Some college, no degree**	**Associate degree**	**Bachelor's degree**	**Master's degree**	**Professional degree**	**Doctorate**	**Bachelor's or higher**	**All workers**
Median earnings										
All employees										
Hispanic	$16,877	$22,289	$26,737	$27,577	$35,556	$47,358	$50,694	—	$38,221	$21,791
White, non-Hispanic	$20,377	$25,954	$30,938	$31,836	$41,979	$50,916	$80,301	$72,353	$46,964	$32,173
Black	$16,046	$21,682	$26,607	$28,152	$38,917	$41,906	$52,210	$60,399	$40,619	$25,832
Asian/Pacific Islander	$17,545	$22,397	$27,356	$31,019	$40,125	$56,779	$73,441	$73,148	$46,504	$31,756
Men	$20,726	$30,658	$35,755	$39,863	$50,730	$61,807	$86,741	$75,004	$55,229	$36,116
Women	$12,990	$19,285	$23,020	$25,810	$33,662	$41,790	$50,308	$51,627	$36,626	$23,865
Total	$17,787	$25,081	$29,902	$31,358	$41,361	$50,703	$76,659	$71,541	$46,025	$30,552
Year-round, full-time employees										
Hispanic	$20,043	$25,893	$30,756	$34,297	$39,888	$50,058	$71,287	—	$42,796	$25,953
White, non-Hispanic	$25,653	$31,047	$36,847	$37,840	$50,661	$57,000	$91,155	$79,395	$54,533	$39,815
Black	$20,096	$25,608	$30,640	$32,950	$41,663	$46,711	$56,412	—	$42,995	$30,395
Asian/Pacific Islander	$20,458	$26,111	$31,354	$35,769	$46,978	$62,337	$77,163	$80,054	$52,346	$38,818
Men	$23,804	$33,036	$40,159	$41,658	$53,108	$66,933	$100,000+	$81,077	$60,553	$40,706
Women	$17,124	$24,216	$28,838	$31,193	$39,818	$48,275	$60,092	$60,425	$42,046	$30,445
Total	$21,552	$29,800	$35,505	$36,783	$48,895	$56,494	$85,920	$77,215	$52,091	$36,311

Source: U.S. Census Bureau (2004a)

Note. Too few Native Americans were included in the sample to produce reliable estimates. High school diploma includes GED or high school equivalency. Empty cells indicate too few cases to produce reliable estimates.

Figure 3.1

Life Earnings Estimates for Full-Time, Year-Round Workers by Gender and Education (based on 1997–1999 work experience)

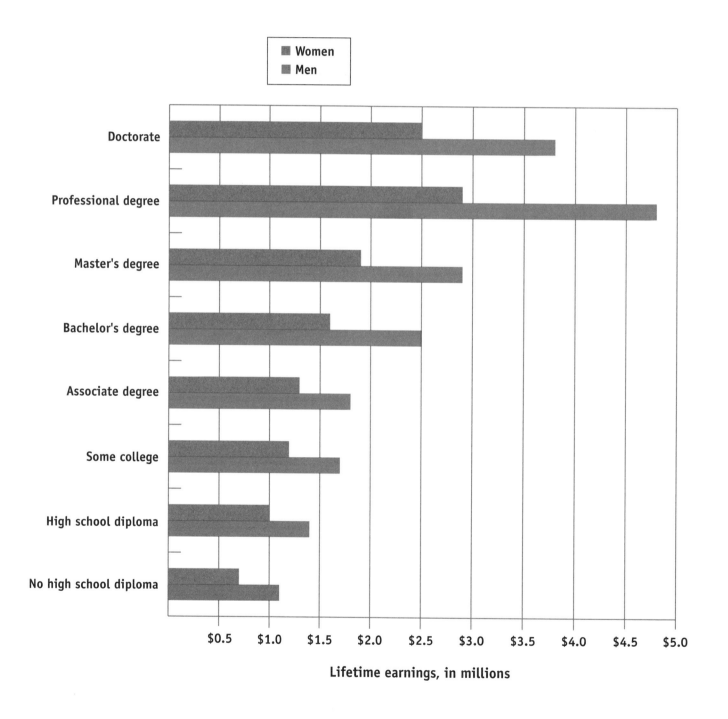

Lifetime earnings, in millions

Source: U.S. Census Bureau (2002)

Table 3.4

Mean Earnings of Workers Aged 25 or Older, by Highest Level of Education Attained: 1994–2002

Highest Level of Education Attained	Year									% change 1994–1998	% change 1998–2002	% change 1994–2002
	1994	1995	1996	1997	1998	1999	2000	2001	2002			
Current dollars												
Less than 9th grade	$15,191	$14,021	$15,043	$16,214	$17,070	$16,928	$18,394	$18,519	$18,935	12%	11%	25%
9–12 grade, no diploma	$15,982	$17,009	$18,384	$19,621	$18,913	$19,474	$22,076	$22,969	$22,463	18%	19%	41%
High school diploma	$21,836	$23,063	$23,946	$24,711	$25,257	$26,527	$27,978	$28,816	$29,185	16%	16%	34%
Some college, no degree	$24,747	$26,760	$28,720	$29,550	$30,571	$32,267	$33,945	$34,567	$35,370	24%	16%	43%
Associate degree	$27,681	$29,033	$29,702	$31,218	$33,765	$33,506	$35,103	$35,972	$35,590	22%	5%	29%
Bachelor's degree	$38,947	$38,574	$39,525	$41,904	$45,390	$47,423	$51,649	v52,462	$53,103	17%	17%	36%
Master's degree	$46,536	$47,785	$50,362	$51,362	$52,951	$55,922	$61,295	$63,823	$60,726	14%	15%	30%
Professional degree	$82,749	$85,601	$94,130	$95,521	$95,954	$102,014	$95,150	$101,728	$113,242	16%	18%	37%
Doctorate	$67,909	$64,654	$72,464	$77,505	$75,071	$86,985	$80,223	$85,675	$89,638	11%	19%	32%
Total	$28,645	$29,579	$31,054	$32,536	$34,068	$35,824	$38,068	$39,378	$39,849	19%	17%	39%
Constant 2002 dollars												
Less than 9th grade	$18,233	$16,430	$17,167	$18,116	$18,808	$18,267	$19,208	$18,814	$18,935	3%	1%	4%
9–12 grade, no diploma	$19,183	$19,931	$20,979	$21,923	$20,839	$21,015	$23,053	$23,334	$22,463	9%	8%	17%
High school diploma	$26,209	$27,026	$27,327	$27,610	$27,828	$28,626	$29,216	$29,274	$29,185	6%	5%	11%
Some college, no degree	$29,703	$31,358	$32,775	$33,017	$33,683	$34,820	$35,447	$35,117	$35,370	13%	5%	19%
Associate degree	$33,225	$34,021	$33,895	$34,881	$37,203	$36,157	$36,657	$36,544	$35,590	12%	-4%	7%
Bachelor's degree	$46,747	$45,201	$45,105	$46,820	$50,011	$51,175	$53,935	$53,296	$53,103	7%	6%	14%
Master's degree	$55,856	$55,995	$57,472	$57,388	$58,342	$60,346	$64,008	$64,838	$60,726	4%	4%	9%
Professional degree	$99,322	$100,308	$107,419	$106,728	$105,723	$110,084	$99,361	$103,346	$113,242	6%	7%	14%
Doctorate	$81,509	$75,762	$82,694	$86,598	$82,714	$93,866	$83,774	$87,038	$89,638	1%	8%	10%
Total	$34,382	$34,661	$35,438	$36,353	$37,536	$38,658	$39,753	$40,004	$39,849	9%	6%	16%

Source: U.S. Census Bureau (1998, 1999, 2000, 2002, 2004a)

Note. High school diploma includes GED or high school equivalency.

Table 3.5

Certificates and Degrees Awarded by Title IV Colleges: 1994–2002

Certificates and Degrees Awarded	Academic Year							Change 1994–1995 to 2001–2002	% change 1994–1995 to 2001–2002
	1994–1995	1995–1996	1996–1997	1997–1998	1999–2000	2000–2001	2001–2002		
Pre-baccalaureate									
Less than 2-year certificate	481,257	483,326	508,954	493,597	525,853	533,398	586,538	105,281	21.9%
Associate degree	527,752	530,457	547,596	553,352	562,929	582,945	599,479	71,727	13.6%
Greater than 2, but less than 4-year certificate	32,402	31,699	32,639	32,576	27,020	26,017	27,666	-4,736	-14.6%
Total pre-baccalaureate awarded	1,041,411	1,045,482	1,089,189	1,079,525	1,115,802	1,142,360	1,213,683	172,272	16.5%
Post-baccalaureate									
Bachelor's degree	1,162,013	1,167,446	1,176,174	1,191,083	1,245,806	1,307,455	1,364,132	202,119	17.4%
Post-baccalaureate certificate	7,853	8,529	7,955	7,953	13,405	15,486	16,974	9,121	116.1%
Master's degree	394,244	403,569	416,825	430,210	456,603	471,166	487,602	93,358	23.7%
Post-master's certificate	8,368	8,525	8,629	8,768	8,948	9,513	10,532	2,164	25.9%
Doctorate	43,792	44,162	45,544	45,823	44,511	44,916	44,198	406	0.9%
First professional degree	75,353	75,966	77,898	78,116	79,201	80,395	81,279	5,926	7.9%
First professional certificate	415	694	495	676	835	729	800	385	92.8%
Total post-baccalaureate awarded	530,025	541,445	557,346	571,546	603,503	622,205	641,385	111,360	21.0%

Source: NCES (2004c)

Note. Includes all colleges eligible for Federal Title IV Student Financial Aid participation. Data are unavailable for 1998–1999.

Figure 3.2

Percentage of Community College Certificates and Associate Degrees Awarded, by Race/Ethnicity: 2001–2002

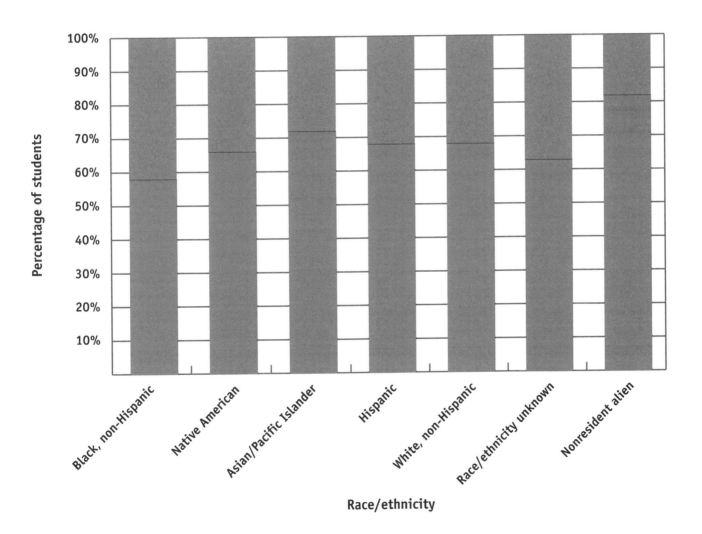

Legend:
- ■ Certificates
- ■ Associate degrees

Y-axis: Percentage of students

X-axis categories: Black, non-Hispanic; Native American; Asian/Pacific Islander; Hispanic; White, non-Hispanic; Race/ethnicity unknown; Nonresident alien

X-axis label: Race/ethnicity

Source: NCES (2004c)

Table 3.6

**Community College Certificates and Degrees Awarded,
by State/Jurisdiction: 2001–2002**

State/Jurisdiction	Certificates Less than 1 year	1–2 years	More than 2 but less than 4 years	Total	Associate degrees
Alabama	2,277	2,124	56	4,457	6,310
Alaska	46	152	0	198	858
American Samoa	0	2	0	2	174
Arizona	8,686	4,343	0	13,029	8,024
Arkansas	2,007	1,074	2	3,083	3,794
California	13,209	13,307	1,964	28,480	77,675
Colorado	2,564	1,786	0	4,350	4,888
Connecticut	698	37	0	735	3,546
Delaware	350	310	0	660	969
Florida	16,158	3,872	84	20,114	38,480
Georgia	10,442	3,690	1,509	15,641	6,822
Guam	8	46	0	54	125
Hawaii	47	358	0	405	2,687
Idaho	329	655	165	1,149	4,318
Illinois	12,613	4,691	0	17,304	22,778
Indiana	76	1,560	0	1,636	4,588
Iowa	1,244	2,678	7	3,929	9,433
Kansas	2,942	1,199	55	4,196	6,569
Kentucky	3,699	1,610	8	5,317	4,558
Louisiana	1,327	469	12	1,808	2,366
Maine	48	287	58	393	1,575
Marshall Islands	0	0	0	0	35
Maryland	0	1,707	0	1,707	7,364
Massachusetts	1,379	691	0	2,070	12,819
Michigan	823	4,331	473	5,627	14,332
Micronesia	0	60	22	82	176
Minnesota	2,729	5,190	1,016	8,935	10,108
Mississippi	222	1,615	83	1,920	6,933

| | Certificates | | | | Associate degrees |
	Less than 1 year	1–2 years	More than 2 but less than 4 years	Total	
Missouri	1,065	1,037	25	2,127	7,314
Montana	5	200	2	207	1,361
Nebraska	614	651	2	1,267	3,423
Nevada	0	252	0	252	2,056
New Hampshire	465	186	0	651	2,161
New Jersey	220	644	0	864	11,280
New Mexico	466	793	35	1,294	3,436
New York	669	1,741	70	2,480	40,533
North Carolina	9,419	3,338	2	12,759	13,927
North Dakota	45	380	3	428	1,746
Northern Marianas Islands	0	0	0	0	82
Ohio	3,027	1,725	2	4,754	15,668
Oklahoma	163	342	0	505	6,318
Oregon	244	1,169	60	1,473	5,972
Palau	0	0	26	26	32
Pennsylvania	5,131	1,112	281	6,524	12,262
Puerto Rico	30	94	0	124	1,064
Rhode Island	25	147	0	172	1,916
South Carolina	4,203	1,231	114	5,548	6,211
South Dakota	102	373	242	717	1,297
Tennessee	807	479	0	1,286	5,991
Texas	6,328	11,118	575	18,021	28,358
Utah	358	587	11	956	6,898
Vermont	0	116	0	116	766
Virginia	2,924	1,822	0	4,746	10,552
Washington	4,421	3,621	626	8,668	19,461
West Virginia	1	135	0	136	2,156
Wisconsin	8,558	3,273	433	12,264	10,065
Wyoming	36	314	3	353	1,683
Grand Total	133,249	94,724	8,026	235,999	486,293

Source: NCES (2004c)

Table 3.7

Community College Certificates and Degrees Awarded, by Field of Study: 2001–2002

Field of Study	Certificates	Associate Degrees
Agricultural business and production	3,852	3,794
Agricultural sciences	155	814
Architecture and related programs	9	339
Area, ethnic, and cultural studies	280	93
Biological/life sciences	101	1,477
Business management and administrative services	37,109	71,515
Communications	409	1,978
Communications technologies	808	1,878
Computer and information sciences	9,873	17,590
Conservation and renewable natural resources	1,018	1,214
Construction trades	8,598	2,337
Consumer and personal services	9,875	3,781
Education	2,003	8,348
Engineering	78	1,586
Engineering-related technologies	8,019	19,164
English language and literature/letters	179	839
Foreign languages and literatures	288	508
Health professions and related sciences	64,880	65,197
Home economics	1,355	836
Law and legal studies	1,389	4,410
Liberal arts and sciences, general studies, and humanities	3,659	196,358
Library science	198	94
Marketing operations/marketing and distribution	8,720	4,983
Mathematics	6	672
Mechanics and repairers	18,128	7,952
Multi/interdisciplinary studies	240	12,898
Not classified by field of study	3	135
Parks, recreation, leisure, and fitness studies	658	793

Field of Study	Certificates	Associate Degrees
Philosophy and religion	4	95
Physical sciences	26	1,297
Precision production trades	11,303	6,822
Protective services	17,483	15,103
Psychology	43	1,623
Public administration and services	794	2,999
ROTC and military technologies	0	62
Science technologies	251	839
Social sciences and history	204	5,421
Theological studies/religious vocations	15	9
Transportation and material moving workers	9,987	738
Visual and performing arts	2,465	11,740
Vocational home economics	11,534	7,962
Total awarded	235,999	486,293

Source: NCES (2004c)

Table 3.8

Community College Certificates and Degrees Awarded,
by Gender and Race/Ethnicity: 2001–2002

Gender	Race/Ethnicity							
	Black, non-Hispanic	Native American	Asian/ Pacific Islander	Hispanic	White, non-Hispanic	Race/ ethnicity unknown	Nonresident alien	Total
Number awarded								
Associate degrees								
Men	14,859	1,795	10,478	16,938	127,749	7,691	4,548	184,058
Women	32,626	3,871	15,617	30,820	202,566	10,194	6,541	302,235
Total	47,485	5,666	26,095	47,758	330,315	17,885	11,089	486,293
Certificates								
Men	14,464	1,294	4,533	10,450	74,187	5,583	994	111,505
Women	19,934	1,617	5,635	12,454	78,338	5,055	1,461	124,494
Total	34,398	2,911	10,168	22,904	152,525	10,638	2,455	235,999
Percentage awarded								
Associate degrees								
Men	8.1%	1.0%	5.7%	9.2%	69.4%	4.2%	2.5%	100.0%
Women	10.8%	1.3%	5.2%	10.2%	67.0%	3.4%	2.2%	100.0%
Total	9.8%	1.2%	5.4%	9.8%	67.9%	3.7%	2.3%	100.0%
Certificates								
Men	13.0%	1.2%	4.1%	9.4%	66.5%	5.0%	0.9%	100.0%
Women	16.0%	1.3%	4.5%	10.0%	62.9%	4.1%	1.2%	100.0%
Total	14.6%	1.2%	4.3%	9.7%	64.6%	4.5%	1.0%	100.0%

Source: NCES (2004c)

Figure 3.3
Main Purpose for Enrolling for 1995–1996 Beginning Community College Students

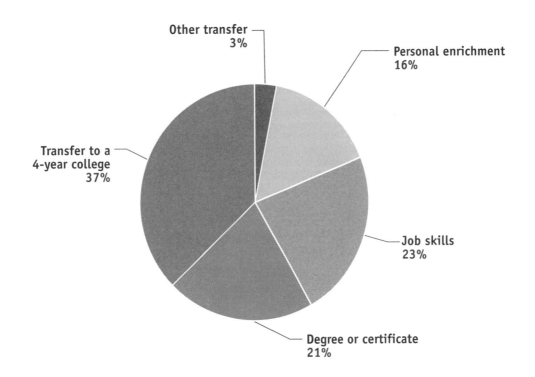

Source: Hoachlander, Sikora, & Horn (2003, Table 3)

Table 3.9

June 2001 Award and Persistence Status of Undergraduates Entering College 1995–1996, by Highest Degree Expected and College Type

Highest Degree Expected in 1995–1996	Award Attained				No Award Attained		
	Bachelor's degree	Associate degree	Certificate	Any award	Enrolled at a 4-year college	Enrolled at less than a 4-year college	Not enrolled
Public community college							
Less than bachelor's degree	1.5%	17.1%	12.8%	31.4%	0.5%	6.2%	61.8%
Bachelor's degree	9.3%	16.7%	8.2%	34.2%	10.8%	9.4%	45.6%
Advanced degree	18.5%	15.1%	7.8%	41.4%	12.9%	9.9%	35.7%
Unknown	5.2%	11.0%	14.5%	30.7%	3.7%	12.1%	53.5%
Total	10.3%	15.8%	9.7%	35.8%	8.4%	9.1%	46.8%
Public 4-year college							
Less than bachelor's degree	4.3%	20.3%	8.8%	33.4%	7.0%	3.8%	55.8%
Bachelor's degree	39.6%	6.9%	3.7%	50.2%	14.4%	3.9%	31.6%
Advanced degree	60.0%	2.3%	2.4%	64.7%	14.6%	2.6%	18.1%
Unknown	48.6%	6.0%	3.6%	58.2%	14.5%	2.2%	25.1%
Total	53.0%	4.4%	2.8%	60.2%	14.5%	2.8%	22.5%
Independent nonprofit 4-year college							
Less than bachelor's degree	—	—	—	—	—	—	—
Bachelor's degree	51.5%	4.7%	2.3%	58.5%	9.7%	2.8%	29.0%
Advanced degree	75.2%	2.0%	1.0%	78.2%	7.1%	2.1%	12.6%
Unknown	68.0%	2.9%	2.0%	72.9%	4.6%	0.9%	21.7%
Total	68.9%	2.8%	1.8%	73.5%	7.1%	2.3%	17.1%
Proprietary college							
Less than bachelor's degree	0.0%	4.7%	57.9%	62.6%	0.1%	1.6%	35.7%
Bachelor's degree	3.7%	11.1%	44.7%	59.5%	1.4%	2.2%	37.0%
Advanced degree	3.3%	16.1%	41.9%	61.3%	4.6%	5.0%	29.2%
Unknown	1.5%	7.8%	45.9%	55.2%	0.0%	1.2%	43.6%
Total	4.4%	23.1%	26.8%	54.3%	2.1%	3.0%	40.6%

Highest Degree Expected in 1995–1996	Award Attained				No Award Attained		
	Bachelor's degree	Associate degree	Certificate	Any award	Enrolled at public 4-year college	Enrolled at independent 4-year college	Not enrolled
Other[a]							
Less than bachelor's degree	0.0%	7.8%	46.0%	53.8%	0.0%	6.0%	40.2%
Bachelor's degree	3.5%	17.9%	30.0%	51.4%	7.4%	8.7%	32.5%
Advanced degree	17.3%	15.0%	34.6%	66.9%	4.0%	4.3%	24.8%
Unknown	0.7%	7.7%	43.6%	52.0%	0.6%	2.8%	44.5%
Total	1.1%	3.7%	56.3%	61.1%	1.1%	2.9%	35.0%
All colleges							
Less than bachelor's degree	1.2%	7.9%	28.5%	37.6%	0.6%	4.7%	52.5%
Bachelor's degree	18.1%	12.6%	10.7%	41.4%	10.4%	7.1%	40.4%
Advanced degree	46.6%	13.3%	5.7%	65.6%	11.8%	5.1%	23.4%
Unknown	23.6%	7.3%	17.5%	48.4%	5.6%	5.6%	39.9%
Total	28.8%	10.0%	12.1%	50.9%	8.8%	5.6%	34.7%

Source: NCES (2004b)

[a]Includes less than 2-year and private nonprofit community colleges.

Table 3.10

Percentage of 1995–1996 Beginning Community College Students Who Attained Degrees at or Attended 4-Year Colleges, by Degree Expectation and Purpose

Degree Expectation and Enrollment Purpose in 1995–1996	Attained degree or certificate	Status of 4-Year Students Not Attaining a Degree or Certificate			Total attending 4 years or attaining degrees
		Attended, still enrolled	Attended, no longer enrolled	Total attended	
Degree expectation in community college					
None	21.2%	8.2%	5.1%	13.4%	34.5%
Any credential or transfer	38.8%	8.2%	4.0%	12.2%	51.0%
Certificate	42.3%	0.0%	0.0%	0.0%	42.4%
Associate degree	37.8%	7.2%	3.2%	10.4%	48.2%
Transfer to 4-year college	39.2%	13.9%	7.2%	21.1%	60.4%
Enrollment purpose					
Job skills	30.1%	3.5%	1.2%	4.7%	34.9%
Degree or certificate	36.0%	7.2%	1.9%	9.1%	45.1%
Transfer to 4-year institution	43.0%	14.0%	6.4%	20.4%	63.4%
Other[a]	33.5%	8.9%	4.0%	12.8%	46.3%

Source: Hoachlander, Sikora, & Horn (2003, Table 7b)

[a]Includes transfer to other community college and transfer for personal enrichment.

Figure 3.4

Distribution of 1995–1996 Beginning Community College Students, by Highest Degree Expected: Degree Attainment and Persistence Status as of June 2001

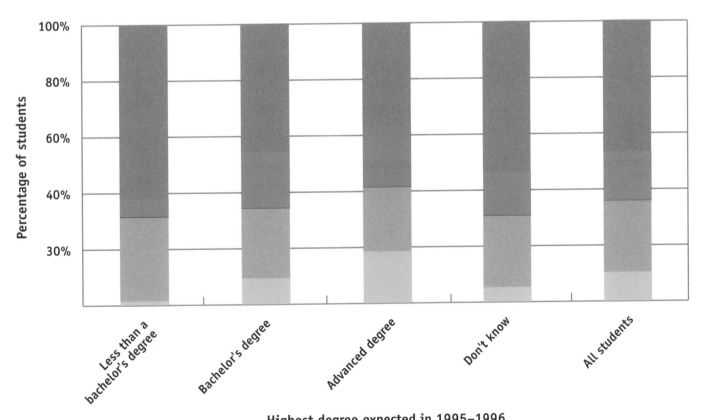

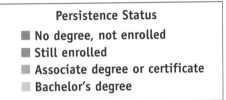

Persistence Status
- No degree, not enrolled
- Still enrolled
- Associate degree or certificate
- Bachelor's degree

Percentage of students

Highest degree expected in 1995–1996

Source: NCES (2004b)

Figure 3.5

Percentage of 1995–1996 Beginning Community College Students
Who Transferred to a 4-Year College, by Degree Expectation

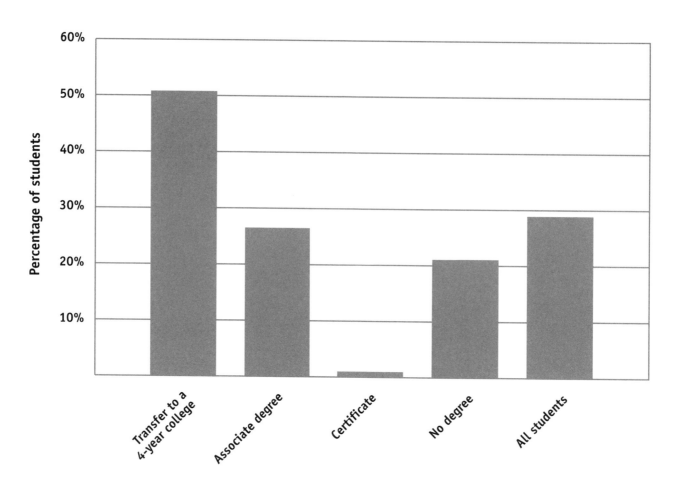

Highest degree expected in 1995–1996

Source: NCES (2004b)

Table 3.11

Percentage of 1995–1996 Beginning Community College Students Who Transferred to a 4-Year College: Degree Attainment and Persistence Status as of 2001, by Degree Expectation

Degree Expectation in 1995–1996	Transferred to 4-year college	Degree Attainment and Persistence Status of Transfer Students as of 2001			
		Attained bachelor's degree	Still enrolled in 4-year college	Total persisted in 4-year college	Attained associate degrees
Transfer to a 4-year college	50.8%	44.0%	38.3%	82.3%	18.8%
Associate degree	26.5%	29.1%	49.5%	78.6%	50.6%
Certificate	1.0%	—	—	—	—
No degree	21.1%	27.6%	45.2%	72.8%	19.4%
Total	28.9%	34.7%	44.3%	78.9%	33.3%

Source: Hoachlander, Sikora, & Horn (2003, Table 8)

Note. Empty cells indicate too few cases to produce reliable estimates.

Table 3.12

Top 15 Hot Programs at Community Colleges: 2004

Program	% of programs	Program Statistics Average starting salary	Average # of students
1. Registered nursing	19.6%	$38,416	170
2. Law enforcement	5.7%	$31,865	179
3. Licensed practical nursing	5.1%	$27,507	98
4. Radiology	4.6%	$35,612	72
5. Computer technologies	3.7%	$35,469	778
6. Automotive	3.5%	$32,498	162
7. Nursing assistant	3.1%	$16,754	140
8. Dental hygiene	2.9%	$35,956	59
9. Health information technology	2.6%	$26,578	54
10. Construction	2.5%	$34,414	223
11. Education	2.4%	$30,810	297
12. Business	2.2%	$31,366	506
13. Networking	2.1%	$35,938	64
14. Electronics	1.7%	$32,734	58
15. Medical assistant	1.7%	$22,953	121

Source: McPhee (2004)

Note. Hot programs are those in which students, according to reporting colleges, are in high demand upon graduation. Data pertain to both for-credit and noncredit programs.

Table 3.13

Top 10 Hot Programs at Community Colleges,
by Starting Salary: 2004

Program	Starting Salary		
	Average	Minimum	Maximum
1. Computer programming	$48,500	$32,000	$65,000
2. Manufacturing	$40,178	$22,000	$65,000
3. Cardiovascular technology	$40,000	$40,000	$40,000
4. Homeland security	$40,000	$35,000	$45,000
5. Cybersecurity	$38,625	$35,000	$50,000
6. Engineering	$38,451	$29,000	$55,000
8. Registered nursing	$38,416	$18,000	$72,000
9. Real estate	$38,093	$20,000	$60,000
10. Occupational therapy assistant	$38,000	$38,000	$38,000
11. Mortuary science	$36,666	$30,000	$45,000

Source: McPhee (2004)

Note. Hot programs are those in which students, according to reporting colleges, are in high demand upon graduation. Data pertain to both for-credit and noncredit programs.

Table 3.14

Top 15 For-Credit Hot Programs at Community Colleges: 2000 and 2004

Program	Program Statistics		
	% of for-credit programs	Average starting salary	Average # of students
2000			
1. Registered nursing	15.3%	$32,757	128
2. General computer technologies	12.5%	$34,242	221
3. Computer networking	8.2%	$38,678	170
4. Engineering-electric/electronics	5.3%	$29,464	103
5. Computer technician/networking	4.5%	$36,092	122
6. Manufacturing technology	4.1%	$30,292	31
7. Radiology technology	3.3%	$32,478	22
8. Digital media	3.3%	$35,409	172
9. Computer programming	3.3%	$30,838	291
10. General skilled trades	3.1%	$25,598	70
11. Law enforcement	2.7%	$27,975	65
12. Dental hygiene	2.5%	$41,907	37
13. Computer-aided design	2.5%	$27,969	313
14. Automotive	2.5%	$29,306	103
15. General allied health	2.2%	$24,782	53
2004			
1. Registered nursing	26.0%	$38,419	173
2. Licensed practical nursing	6.8%	$27,548	100
3. Radiology	6.2%	$35,623	73
4. Law enforcement	5.8%	$32,949	143
5. Automotive	4.1%	$32,733	73
6. Computer technologies	3.8%	$34,647	437
7. Dental hygiene	3.6%	$36,891	60
8. Education	2.2%	$31,462	343
9. Health information technology	2.2%	$27,481	47
10. Electronics	2.1%	$32,764	43
11. Business	2.0%	$29,247	637
12. Medical lab technician	1.8%	$33,299	39
13. Computer networking	1.7%	$33,039	69
14. Culinary arts	1.6%	$27,961	140
15. Medical assistant	1.5%	$23,983	107

Source: McPhee (2004); Nock & Shults (2001)

Note. Hot programs are those in which students, according to reporting colleges, are in high demand upon graduation.

Table 3.15

Percentage of Baccalaureate Recipients, by Field of Study and Type of College First Attended: 1999–2000

College Type	Field of Study					
	Humanities	Social/ behavioral sciences	Life sciences	Physical sciences	Math	Computer/ information science
Public 4-year college	45.7%	46.7%	51.3%	53.2%	57.8%	45.7%
Public community college	17.0%	18.7%	18.5%	10.8%	7.7%	29.7%
Public college, less-than-2-year	0.2%	0.3%	0.1%	0.1%	0.0%	0.3%
Private nonprofit 4-year college	34.1%	32.3%	28.6%	35.5%	33.9%	21.5%
Private nonprofit community college	1.2%	0.4%	0.7%	0.3%	0.6%	0.1%
Private nonprofit college, less-than-2-year	0.2%	0.1%	0.0%	0.0%	0.0%	0.2%
Private 4-year college	0.3%	0.0%	0.1%	0.0%	0.0%	1.8%
Private community college	0.7%	0.8%	0.6%	0.0%	0.0%	0.0%
Private college, less-than-2-year	0.7%	0.8%	0.0%	0.0%	0.0%	0.7%
% who ever attended a community college	49.2%	46.7%	45.9%	42.6%	38.1%	60.0%

College Type	Field of Study					
	Engineering	Education	Business/ management	Health	Vocational/ technical	Other technical/ professional	Total, all fields
Public 4-year college	57.6%	47.9%	50.4%	52.7%	52.4%	55.8%	49.8%
Public community college	18.4%	26.8%	22.0%	21.4%	22.8%	19.2%	20.2%
Public college, less-than-2-year	0.0%	0.0%	0.3%	0.3%	0.0%	0.1%	0.2%
Private nonprofit 4-year college	22.6%	22.6%	23.1%	21.4%	22.1%	22.8%	27.0%
Private nonprofit community college	0.3%	1.2%	0.6%	2.8%	1.2%	0.5%	0.9%
Private nonprofit college, less-than-2-year	0.0%	0.1%	0.2%	0.1%	0.0%	0.0%	0.1%
Private 4-year college	0.6%	0.3%	1.7%	0.3%	0.0%	0.6%	0.6%
Private community college	0.3%	0.5%	1.0%	0.6%	0.2%	0.4%	0.6%
Private college, less-than-2-year	0.2%	0.6%	0.7%	0.4%	1.4%	0.6%	0.6%
% who ever attended a community college	48.3%	58.3%	57.3%	60.1%	59.2%	50.4%	52.3%

Source: NCES (2004a)

Table 3.16

Number of First-Time Candidates Taking the NCLEX-RN Exam and Percentage Passing, by Credential Earned: 2000–2004

Credential Earned	Time Period and Pass Rate									
	January–March		April–June		July–August		September–December		Full year	
	#	% passing	#	% passing	#	% passing	#	% passing	#	% passing
2000										
Diploma	640	82.3%	455	84.0%	1,301	85.1%	283	77.0%	2,679	83.4%
Baccalaureate	5,332	85.9%	5,331	86.9%	13,796	83.2%	1,589	72.7%	26,048	83.9%
Associate degree	8,260	83.9%	9,838	86.2%	21,544	84.0%	3,023	74.4%	42,665	83.8%
% with associate degree	58.0%	—	63.0%	—	58.8%	—	61.8%	—	59.8%	—
2001										
Diploma	544	85.3%	337	87.8%	1,163	87.6%	266	79.7%	2,310	86.2%
Baccalaureate	5,065	86.7%	4,841	88.3%	13,327	85.9%	1,599	75.4%	24,832	85.9%
Associate degree	7,991	83.7%	8,950	88.1%	21,401	86.3%	3,225	75.0%	41,567	85.3%
% with associate degree	58.8%	—	63.3%	—	59.6%	—	63.4%	—	60.5%	—
2002										
Diploma	551	85.3%	336	87.2%	1,336	86.8%	201	84.6%	2,424	86.3%
Baccalaureate	4,906	87.6%	4,104	88.6%	15,411	86.7%	1,385	77.7%	25,806	86.7%
Associate degree	7,692	86.3%	8,542	55.5%	23,408	86.9%	2,668	75.8%	42,310	86.7%
% with associate degree	58.5%	—	65.8%	—	58.3%	—	62.7%	—	60.0%	—
2003										
Diploma	591	90.0%	466	93.8%	1,276	89.7%	232	81.9%	2,565	89.8%
Baccalaureate	5,277	87.0%	6,425	90.4%	13,141	86.2%	1,787	79.1%	26,630	86.9%
Associate degree	9,010	87.1%	13,283	90.0%	21,832	86.5%	3,298	77.5%	47,423	87.0%
% with associate degree	60.6%	—	65.8%	—	60.2%	—	62.0%	—	61.9%	—

	Time Period and Pass Rate									
	January–March		April–June		July–August		September–December		Full year	
Credential Earned	#	% passing	#	% passing	#	% passing	#	% passing	#	% passing
2004										
Diploma	836	87.2%	498	91.2%	—	—	—	—	—	—
Baccalaureate	6,637	87.2%	7,438	88.2%	—	—	—	—	—	—
Associate degree	10,854	87.0%	14,804	88.2%	—	—	—	—	—	—
% with associate degree	59.2%	—	65.1%	—	—	—	—	—	—	—
Totals, 2000–2004										
Diploma	3,162	86.0%	2,092	88.9%	5,076	87.2%	982	80.3%	9,978	86.3%
Baccalaureate	27,217	86.9%	28,139	88.5%	55,675	85.5%	6,360	76.2%	103,316	85.8%
Associate degree	43,807	85.7%	55,417	80.9%	88,185	85.9%	12,214	75.7%	173,965	85.7%
% with associate degree	59.1%	—	64.7%	—	59.2%	—	62.5%	—	60.6%	—

Source: NCSBN (2004a, 2004b, 2004c, 2004d, 2004e)

Note. NCLEX-RN exam: National Council Licensure Examinations for Registered Nursing. Empty cells indicate that data were not available at the time of publication.

[a]Totals for 2000–2004 exclude 2004 data.

Table 3.17

Teaching Status of 1999–2000 Baccalaureate Recipients, by Type of College First Attended: 2001

Teaching Status	Type of College First Attended						% who ever attended a community college
	Public 4-year college	Public community college	Private nonprofit 4-year college	Private nonprofit community college	Private 4-year college	Private community college	
Sub or aide, not certified, no prep	56.3%	11.9%	30.9%	0.1%	0.0%	0.0%	52.1%
Did not teach/prepare, considered	46.4%	20.4%	29.9%	0.5%	1.1%	0.8%	52.4%
Did not teach, did prepare	47.9%	22.1%	25.1%	1.5%	0.8%	1.9%	53.3%
Taught, not certified, did not prepare	46.5%	19.3%	31.4%	1.1%	0.0%	0.0%	48.0%
Taught, not certified, did prepare	50.9%	22.6%	23.7%	0.8%	0.0%	2.1%	65.5%
Taught, certified	50.7%	22.5%	24.5%	1.2%	0.1%	0.3%	56.9%
Teach full time currently	48.7%	21.9%	27.4%	1.0%	0.1%	0.4%	53.5%
Teach part time currently	54.0%	19.3%	23.1%	1.3%	0.4%	0.5%	57.8%
Employed as a K–12 teacher	49.7%	22.9%	25.6%	0.6%	0.1%	0.5%	56.1%
Taught K–12	50.0%	21.2%	26.4%	1.0%	0.2%	0.4%	54.7%
All 1999–2000 baccalaureate recipients	49.8%	20.2%	27.0%	0.9%	0.6%	0.6%	52.3%

Source: NCES (2004a)

IV

Community College Staff and Services

Community colleges are experiencing a real changing of the guard as the new century progresses. Presidents are retiring in increasing numbers, as are senior administrators, faculty, and support staff. A survey conducted by AACC in 2001 revealed that 45% of presidents intend to retire by 2007 (Shults, 2001). Presidents responding to the survey also noted that at least one fourth of their senior administrators and senior faculty would retire by that time as well.

This situation has both negative and positive consequences. The retirement of such large numbers of dedicated leaders and workers will result in a significant knowledge drain as the collective wisdom of these people, gained through many years of experience, leaves with them. The knowledge drain may be particularly serious with regard to all of the support staff who carry out the day-to-day routines that ensure the effective functioning of colleges. It is also possible that some

of the vacancies caused by retirements will not be filled if budget constraints continue, and this may affect the capacity of colleges to carry out some functions. Perhaps the greatest difficulty arising from the retirement exodus may be the lack of potential leaders in the pipeline, because many of the senior administrators who might have been expected to assume higher-level positions will choose instead to conclude their careers and retire.

The departure of so many people during the next few years, however, also offers an excellent opportunity for colleges to discard outdated practices, create new work patterns, and introduce organizational structures and models that promote greater efficiency. Colleges may reassign resources and develop new programs and services based on the emerging needs of students and communities. Vacancies resulting from retirements may be used to hire or promote energetic new leaders and workers with new ideas that will help colleges respond to the many

changes occurring in contemporary higher education. Finally, colleges will have the opportunity to employ a more diverse faculty and staff that reflect more closely the growing diversity of the student body and the general population.

This diversification is already occurring. Women now constitute nearly 27% of public and private community college presidents, up from 11% in 1991. Numbers of presidents who are minorities have also increased, from 8.6% in 1986 to 19.8% in 2004 (AACC, 2004a). Numbers of women and minorities in the administrative and faculty ranks are growing as well.

Although community college salaries are generally lower than those in four-year colleges and have remained somewhat stagnant during the past few years, partly because of budget restraints, they are still attractive to many educators. In 2004, salaries for presidents of community college systems and districts averaged $182,294, whereas salaries for presidents of single-campus colleges averaged $126,504. Benefits such as housing, automobiles, and retirement plans made compensation packages even more valuable. Compensation for about 7% of presidents was provided by college foundations, which contributed an average of $14,251 to the base salary (Blount & Associates & Lindley, 2005). The chief academic officer in a community college earned an average of $94,490 in 2003–2004, and the chief business officer averaged $88,170. The average earnings of a chief student affairs officer were $82,460, depending on the size of the college.

Faculty salaries in community colleges continue to be lower than those at four-year colleges, but they are catching up. Although not all community colleges have faculty rank and tenure structures, in 2003 those that did reported the average salary for a full-time community college professor as $65,600, as compared to $69,600 for the same rank at a baccalaureate-granting college. Interestingly, instructors at community colleges averaged $38,000 versus $36,200 for those in four-year colleges. Faculty salaries overall show a broad range, with the highest and the lowest figures occurring in the same state ($92,000 average for a full professor in a New York City college versus $27,000 average for an instructor in rural upstate New York).

Gender differentials in salary remain a problem: Male professors at community colleges average $66,030, compared to $62,357 for female professors (American Association of University Professors, 2004). The gap is somewhat smaller for instructors, with men earning $39,499 on average and women earning $38,691. The wave of retirements has helped community colleges to some extent during a period of fiscal restraints because new hires tend to enter at lower ranks and salaries. However, salary compression has been problematic when pay rates for entry levels are increased to address market rates, and these new hires earn almost as much as associate professors who have been at a college for several years. Faculty salaries, like those of presidents and administrators, vary considerably based on the region of the country and the rural or urban location of the college.

Community colleges rely on a mix of full- and part-time faculty in order to offer students the broadest array of courses, with more than two thirds of instructional staff on part-time assignments. It is important to note that, although part-time instructors may outnumber full-time faculty at many colleges, the majority of class sections are still taught by full-timers.

The adjunct instructors generally teach one or two courses per semester and earn between $2,000 and $3,000 per course. Some teach part time by choice while raising children or holding another full-time job, and some accept part-time positions in the hope of eventually becoming full-time faculty. In many cases, adjunct instructors teach at more than one college during the same semester.

Students benefit from the use of part-time faculty in several ways. Many of the adjunct instructors have business and industry experience that adds a real-life element to their teaching and may provide students with valuable contacts and internships. Talented and dedicated adjunct instructors can also be a real asset when they bring highly specialized skills in rapidly growing fields such as some specialized allied health and emerging technologies fields for which full-time faculty might be very difficult to recruit. And, despite their many time commitments, adjuncts often make themselves available outside of class, just as full-time faculty do, to work with students and support their learning. Colleges are able to offer a greater selection of courses and sections while keeping overall instructional costs low by using highly qualified, temporary, non-salaried instructors.

However, concerns have been raised regarding the growing use of "perma-temps," as the *New York Times* called adjunct instructors (Berger, 2002). Adjunct instructors in community colleges assert that their jobs are made more difficult because they are frequently hired at the last minute, are usually required to use syllabi and textbooks with which they are unfamiliar, have little or no office space for class preparation and meetings with students, and lack secretarial support and technology. For most adjunct instructors there is little time or incentive to be involved in department meetings, curriculum discussions, student advising, and other work that is expected of full-time faculty. In response, many community colleges have instituted mentoring projects, buddy systems, orientations, professional development sessions, and other services for adjunct instructors.

Because human resources are their greatest assets, community colleges are devoting greater attention to professional development for all faculty, administrators, and staff. Even in times of restricted finances, many colleges try to provide various means for their employees to grow professionally, including tuition reimbursement for advanced studies, attendance at conferences, sabbaticals, and mini-grants for special projects. The concern about

impending retirements has led many colleges to establish leadership training programs such as the Leadership Institute at the College of Lake County (CLC) in Illinois. At CLC, faculty, administrators, and support staff come together in a two-day retreat to learn about the Illinois community college system and the national picture. Personal leadership skills development is also included, and participants prepare a professional development plan to extend their growth activities over time. Another professional development opportunity, the Department Chairs Institute, was initiated in 2003 by the North Carolina State University Department of Adult and Community College Education in cooperation with the North Carolina Community College System.

Nationally there are also excellent leadership programs and professional development opportunities. AACC offers the annual Presidents Academy for new and experienced CEOs and established the Future Leaders Institute for aspiring executive administrators in 2003. A number of the affiliated councils of AACC offer leadership training programs as well. These include the National Institute for Leadership Development (NILD) for aspiring women leaders in community colleges; the National Community College Hispanic Council

Leadership Fellows Program, designed to prepare Latinos and Latinas for the presidency; and the National Council on Black American Affairs Leadership Development Institute for African American Midlevel Administrators. Other councils offer targeted training such as the Summer Institute on Marketing and Public Relations sponsored by the National Council for Marketing and Public Relations and the Presidents' Fundraising Workshop sponsored by the Council for Resource Development.

Perhaps the most significant change in community college programs and services over the past few years has been the learning college movement, which was triggered by Robert Barr and John Tagg in 1995 and further developed by Terry O'Banion, president emeritus of the League for Innovation in the Community College. With the 1997 publication of *A Learning College for the 21st Century*, O'Banion challenged colleges to focus on students' learning, provide learning opportunities through multiple delivery modes and timeframes, reenvision faculty facilitators of learning, and gather data to prove that learning has truly occurred. Also, all members of the college community were to be viewed as learners themselves, as well as contributors to students' learning. The principles O'Banion proposed were not entirely new, but in combination and with a clear emphasis on students' learning, the learning college idea constituted a paradigm shift in education.

The capacity of community colleges to respond strategically to emerging learning needs is further illustrated by their emphasis in other program areas including service learning, welfare-to-work initiatives, and teacher training. Service learning is an approach to education that combines formal study with practical experience as a volunteer. Students who enroll in a service learning program generally take one or more for-credit courses in which they study the concepts of service, civic responsibility, and volunteerism; engage in a supervised service activity in the local community; and reflect on their experiences. Such programs allow students to earn credits toward a degree, gain valuable work experience, and examine their roles in resolving societal problems while also benefiting the agencies and communities for which they volunteer.

More than ever, community colleges are seen as the engines of workforce preparation and economic growth. In addition to preparing the general population for work through for-credit and noncredit courses, their welfare-to-work pro-

grams continue to help poor and undereducated people gain job skills so that they can exit the public assistance system and become productive members of society. For example, the Work and Learn Center at Monroe Community College in Rochester, New York, offers a variety of training options and services to more than 3,000 clients each year. The California Community Colleges Chancellor's Office and several other sponsors spearheaded another such program, Building Individual and Community Self-Sufficiency Through Service. California welfare recipients enroll in AmeriCorps, take early childhood courses, and gain work experience in child-care centers, some of which are on community college campuses.

One of the newest programmatic efforts in community colleges addresses the nation's critical shortage of teachers. Community colleges have traditionally offered courses in areas such as elementary education and early childhood education, with the expectation that students will transfer into baccalaureate-level teacher training programs. Additional formal articulation arrangements have been established recently, including the Maryland initiative to offer the associate of arts in teaching at all 19 of its community colleges, with guaranteed admission to a state university

teacher training baccalaureate program upon completion of the two-year degree. Other states have common course-numbering systems or common general education core curricula that accelerate teacher training, and some two-year colleges, such as Miami Dade College, have established separate schools of education that can now offer bachelor's degrees.

There is no doubt that community colleges make a major difference in their local areas by providing high-quality instruction through degree programs and certificates, for-credit courses, and noncredit offerings. Moreover, the impact of these colleges extends far beyond their academic programs when their many community services are taken into account. According to *The Knowledge Net: Connecting Communities, Learners, and Colleges*, "Community colleges must serve all segments of the community. This includes the civic sector, the employer community, and the education sector" (AACC/ACCT, 2000). In addition to the workforce training and service learning programs mentioned earlier, faculty and staff are regularly involved with many other outreach efforts that benefit local residents. Many colleges are also creating new services that help the growing Hispanic population in their target areas adapt to

American society. The Centro Communitario at Brunswick Community College in North Carolina is an excellent example of a partnership with the local community and the Mexican government.

Community colleges are fully engaged with local school districts as well. Many offer tech programs with nearby high schools under the Carl D. Perkins Vocational and Technical Education Act, as well as dual-enrollment programs in which high school students can get a head start on their college studies. Still other colleges have established partnership programs in specialized career fields, such as the online bridge program in nursing at Olive-Harvey College in Chicago and the Valdez Math Institute for high schoolers at San Joaquin Delta College.

Middle schools are receiving more attention as well, because colleges recognize that families and students need to begin planning for higher education at the earliest possible moment. Funded by federal dollars, GEAR UP (Gaining Early Awareness and Readiness for Undergraduate Programs) has been implemented on numerous campuses to help low-income youth prepare for eventual college studies. Math and science and career-focused programs are directed to this age level in colleges across the country, in the hope that as middle school students become comfortable with the college environment they will see a college degree as a goal worth achieving.

As has always been the case, community college programs and

services to their communities offer far more than courses and degrees. These colleges, and all those who work in them, are dedicated to the well-being of their local areas. To that end, members of the surrounding communities can take advantage of day-care centers, career counseling, cultural and sports events, ethnic festivals, political debates, drug education, parenting classes, senior citizens programs, and theater and music troupes, among a host of services. And most campus facilities can be used by the college's friends and neighbors. Through the dedication of their faculty and staffs and their programs and services, community colleges make vital contributions to the intellectual and economic capital and the overall quality of life in their communities. ⊕

Table 4.1

Occupations of Community College Employees, by Employment Status and Gender: 2001

Occupation	Employment Status			Gender			
	Full time	Part time	% full time	Men	Women	% men	Total
Public colleges							
Professional staff							
Faculty	109,183	219,331	33.2%	167,535	160,979	49.0%	328,514
Executive/administrative/managerial	21,470	1,208	95.9%	11,344	11,052	49.3%	22,396
Instruction/research assistant	0	926	0.0%	548	660	54.6%	1,208
Other administrative	5,381	793	87.2%	2,437	3,737	60.5%	6,174
Other professional (support services)	33,507	12,104	73.5%	16,705	28,906	63.4%	45,611
Total	169,541	234,362	42.0%	198,569	205,334	50.8%	403,903
Nonprofessional staff							
Technical and paraprofessional	27,773	16,149	63.2%	16,948	26,974	61.4%	43,922
Clerical and secretarial	53,350	31,208	63.1%	12,038	72,520	85.8%	84,558
Skilled crafts	5,391	1,353	79.9%	5,682	1,062	15.7%	6,744
Service/maintenance	24,283	8,418	74.3%	23,205	9,496	29.0%	32,701
Total	110,797	57,128	66.0%	57,873	110,052	65.5%	167,925
Total public college staff	280,338	291,490	49.0%	256,442	315,386	55.2%	571,828
Independent colleges							
Professional staff							
Faculty	2,777	2,928	48.7%	2,836	2,869	50.3%	5,705
Executive/administrative/managerial	1,082	26	91.6%	537	644	54.5%	1,181
Instruction/research assistant	0	99	0.0%	7	19	73.1%	26
Other administrative	808	175	82.2%	357	626	63.7%	983
Other professional (support services)	1,342	249	84.3%	549	1,042	65.5%	1,591
Total	6,009	3,477	63.3%	4,286	5,200	54.8%	9,486
Nonprofessional staff							
Technical and paraprofessional	484	288	62.7%	202	570	73.8%	772
Clerical and secretarial	1,159	12	99.0%	131	1,040	88.8%	1,171
Skilled crafts	57	182	23.8%	156	83	34.7%	239
Service/maintenance	568	3,959	12.5%	2,131	2,396	52.9%	4,527
Total	2,268	4,441	33.8%	2,620	4,089	60.9%	6,709
Total independent college staff	8,277	12,236	40.4%	8,475	12,038	58.7%	20,513

Occupation	Employment Status			Gender			
	Full time	Part time	% full time	Men	Women	% men	Total
All community colleges							
Professional staff							
Faculty	111,960	222,259	33.5%	170,371	163,848	49.0%	334,219
Executive/administrative/managerial	22,552	1,234	95.7%	11,881	11,696	49.6%	23,577
Instruction/research assistant	0	1,025	0.0%	555	679	55.0%	1,234
Other administrative	6,189	968	86.5%	2,794	4,363	61.0%	7,157
Other professional (support services)	34,849	12,353	73.8%	17,254	29,948	63.4%	47,202
Total	175,550	237,839	42.5%	202,855	210,534	50.9%	413,389
Nonprofessional staff							
Technical and paraprofessional	28,257	16,437	63.2%	17,150	27,544	61.6%	44,694
Clerical and secretarial	54,509	31,220	63.6%	12,169	73,560	85.8%	85,729
Skilled crafts	5,448	1,535	78.0%	5,838	1,145	16.4%	6,983
Service/maintenance	24,851	12,377	66.8%	25,336	11,892	31.9%	37,228
Total	113,065	61,569	64.7%	60,493	114,141	65.4%	174,634
Total community college staff	288,615	303,726	48.7%	264,917	327,424	55.3%	592,341

Source: NCES (2004f)

Table 4.2

Full-Time Employees at Public Community Colleges, by Faculty Status and Occupation: Fall 2001

Occupation	Faculty Status				Total full-time employees
	Tenured	Nontenured, on tenure track	Not on tenure track	No faculty status	
Instruction combined with research/public service	27,992	12,496	141,148	12,104	193,740
Primarily instruction	1,771	449	8,173	186	10,579
Primarily research	4	0	9	27	40
Primarily public service (e.g., extension)	51	0	1,073	1,565	2,689
Executive/administrative	263	47	1,121	13,091	14,522
Other administrative	63	4	521	3,518	4,106
Other professional (e.g., library)	222	181	2,522	20,558	23,483
Technical/paraprofessional	0	0	0	27,160	27,160
Clerical and secretarial	0	0	0	49,596	49,596
Skilled crafts	0	0	0	3,871	3,871
Service/maintenance	0	0	0	19,757	19,757
Total	30,366	13,177	154,567	151,433	349,543

Source: NCES (2004d)

Table 4.3

New Hires in Public Community Colleges, by Occupation and Gender: 2001

Occupation	New Hires				Total staff	% new hires
	Men	Women	% men	Total		
Professional staff						
Faculty	3,938	4,357	47.5%	8,295	109,183	7.6%
Executive/administrative/managerial	565	582	49.3%	1,147	21,470	5.3%
Other administrative	154	182	45.8%	336	5,381	6.2%
Other professional (support services)	892	1,617	35.6%	2,509	33,507	7.5%
Total professional staff	5,549	6,738	45.2%	12,287	169,541	7.2%
Nonprofessional staff						
Technical and paraprofessional	901	1,205	42.8%	2,106	27,773	7.6%
Clerical and secretarial	435	3,343	11.5%	3,778	53,350	7.1%
Skilled crafts	185	44	80.8%	229	5,391	4.2%
Service/maintenance	1,109	435	71.8%	1,544	24,283	6.4%
Total nonprofessional staff	2,630	5,027	34.3%	7,657	110,797	6.9%
Total new hires	8,179	11,765	41.0%	19,944	280,338	7.1%

Source: NCES (2004f)

Table 4.4

Public Community College Staff by Employment Status, Occupation, and Race/Ethnicity: 2001

Employment Status and Occupation	Black	Native American	Asian	Hispanic	Total minority	White	Non-resident alien	Unknown	Total
Number of all full-time staff									
Professional staff									
Faculty	6,835	822	3,812	4,931	16,400	90,330	508	1,572	108,810
Executive/administrative/managerial	2,015	338	512	1,176	4,041	17,218	14	123	21,396
Other administrative	483	122	97	160	862	4,474	12	31	5,379
Other professional (support services)	4,215	348	898	2,104	7,565	25,573	83	170	33,391
Total	13,548	1,630	5,319	8,371	28,868	137,595	617	1,896	168,976
Nonprofessional staff									
Technical and paraprofessional	2,979	393	1,252	2,715	7,339	20,107	65	211	27,722
Clerical and secretarial	6,441	594	1,909	5,702	14,646	38,238	68	270	53,222
Skilled crafts	517	76	128	549	1,270	4,078	13	27	5,388
Service/maintenance	5,589	306	914	3,434	10,243	13,726	67	139	24,175
Total	15,526	1,369	4,203	12,400	33,498	76,149	213	647	110,507
Total full-time staff	29,074	2,999	9,522	20,771	62,366	213,744	830	2,543	279,483
Number of new-hire full-time staff									
Professional staff									
Faculty	500	74	344	422	1,340	6,679	193	83	8,295
Executive/administrative/managerial	114	23	29	72	238	888	21	0	1,147
Other administrative	27	18	6	15	66	269	1	0	336
Other professional (support services)	311	26	79	171	587	1,859	44	19	2,509
Total	952	141	458	680	2,231	9,695	259	102	12,287
Nonprofessional staff									
Technical and paraprofessional	222	47	149	250	668	1,375	56	7	2,106
Clerical and secretarial	493	42	219	473	1,227	2,481	62	8	3,778
Skilled crafts	20	4	8	29	61	166	2	0	229
Service/maintenance	342	31	67	204	644	880	19	1	1,544
Total	1,077	124	443	956	2,600	4,902	139	16	7,657
Total new-hire full-time staff	2,029	265	901	1,636	4,831	14,597	398	118	19,944

Employee Status and Occupation	Race/Ethnicity								
	Black	Native American	Asian	Hispanic	Total minority	White	Non-resident alien	Unknown	Total
Number of part-time staff									
Professional staff									
Faculty	14,888	1,329	5,869	10,123	32,209	167,991	1,330	17,368	218,898
Executive/administrative/managerial	133	47	19	49	248	608	11	108	975
Other administrative	100	11	17	55	183	665	3	17	868
Other professional (support services)	53	2	8	16	79	624	1	89	793
Total	15,174	1,389	5,913	10,243	32,719	169,888	1,345	17,582	221,534
Nonprofessional staff									
Technical and paraprofessional	1,398	53	219	872	2,542	8,814	139	595	12,090
Clerical and secretarial	1,927	142	867	1,362	4,298	10,636	215	998	16,147
Skilled crafts	4,791	266	1,114	3,692	9,863	19,606	594	1,009	31,072
Service/maintenance	136	7	77	72	292	1,014	4	43	1,353
Total	8,252	468	2,277	5,998	16,995	40,070	952	2,645	60,662
Total part-time staff	23,426	1,857	8,190	16,241	49,714	209,958	2,297	20,227	282,196
Percentage of full-time staff									
Professional staff									
Faculty	6.3%	0.8%	3.5%	4.5%	15.1%	83.0%	0.5%	1.4%	100.0%
Executive/administrative/managerial	9.4%	1.6%	2.4%	5.5%	18.9%	80.5%	0.1%	0.6%	100.0%
Other administrative	9.0%	2.3%	1.8%	3.0%	16.0%	83.2%	0.2%	0.6%	100.0%
Other professional (support services)	12.6%	1.0%	2.7%	6.3%	22.7%	76.6%	0.2%	0.5%	100.0%
Total	8.0%	1.0%	3.1%	5.0%	17.1%	81.4%	0.4%	1.1%	100.0%
Nonprofessional staff									
Technical and paraprofessional	10.7%	1.4%	4.5%	9.8%	26.5%	72.5%	0.2%	0.8%	100.0%
Clerical and secretarial	12.1%	1.1%	3.6%	10.7%	27.5%	71.8%	0.1%	0.5%	100.0%
Skilled crafts	9.6%	1.4%	2.4%	10.2%	23.6%	75.7%	0.2%	0.5%	100.0%
Service/maintenance	23.1%	1.3%	3.8%	14.2%	42.4%	56.8%	0.3%	0.6%	100.0%
Total	14.0%	1.2%	3.8%	11.2%	30.3%	68.9%	0.2%	0.6%	100.0%
Total % of full-time staff	10.4%	1.1%	3.4%	7.4%	22.3%	76.5%	0.3%	0.9%	100.0%

Table 4.4 (cont'd)

Public Community College Staff by Employment Status, Occupation, and Race/Ethnicity: 2001

Employee Status and Occupation	Race/Ethnicity								
	Black	Native American	Asian	Hispanic	Total minority	White	Non-resident alien	Unknown	Total
Percentage of new-hire full-time staff									
Professional staff									
Faculty	6.0%	0.9%	4.1%	5.1%	16.2%	80.5%	2.3%	1.0%	100.0%
Executive/administrative/managerial	9.9%	2.0%	2.5%	6.3%	20.7%	77.4%	1.8%	0.0%	100.0%
Other administrative	8.0%	5.4%	1.8%	4.5%	19.6%	80.1%	0.3%	0.0%	100.0%
Other professional (support services)	12.4%	1.0%	3.1%	6.8%	23.4%	74.1%	1.8%	0.8%	100.0%
Total	7.7%	1.1%	3.7%	5.5%	18.2%	78.9%	2.1%	0.8%	100.0%
Nonprofessional staff									
Technical and paraprofessional	10.5%	2.2%	7.1%	11.9%	31.7%	65.3%	2.7%	0.3%	100.0%
Clerical and secretarial	13.0%	1.1%	5.8%	12.5%	32.5%	65.7%	1.6%	0.2%	100.0%
Skilled crafts	8.7%	1.7%	3.5%	12.7%	26.6%	72.5%	0.9%	0.0%	100.0%
Service/maintenance	22.2%	2.0%	4.3%	13.2%	41.7%	57.0%	1.2%	0.1%	100.0%
Total	14.1%	1.6%	5.8%	12.5%	34.0%	64.0%	1.8%	0.2%	100.0%
Total % of new-hire full-time staff	10.2%	1.3%	4.5%	8.2%	24.2%	73.2%	2.0%	0.6%	100.0%
Percentage of part-time staff									
Professional staff									
Faculty	6.8%	0.6%	2.7%	4.6%	14.7%	76.7%	0.6%	7.9%	100.0%
Executive/administrative/managerial	13.6%	4.8%	1.9%	5.0%	25.4%	62.4%	1.1%	11.1%	100.0%
Other administrative	11.5%	1.3%	2.0%	6.3%	21.1%	76.6%	0.3%	2.0%	100.0%
Other professional (support services)	6.7%	0.3%	1.0%	2.0%	10.0%	78.7%	0.1%	11.2%	100.0%
Total	6.8%	0.6%	2.7%	4.6%	14.8%	76.7%	0.6%	7.9%	100.0%
Nonprofessional staff									
Technical and paraprofessional	11.6%	0.4%	1.8%	7.2%	21.0%	72.9%	1.1%	4.9%	100.0%
Clerical and secretarial	11.9%	0.9%	5.4%	8.4%	26.6%	65.9%	1.3%	6.2%	100.0%
Skilled crafts	15.4%	0.9%	3.6%	11.9%	31.7%	63.1%	1.9%	3.2%	100.0%
Service/maintenance	10.1%	0.5%	5.7%	5.3%	21.6%	74.9%	0.3%	3.2%	100.0%
Total	13.6%	0.8%	3.8%	9.9%	28.0%	66.1%	1.6%	4.4%	100.0%
Total % of part-time staff	8.3%	0.7%	2.9%	5.8%	17.6%	74.4%	0.8%	7.2%	100.0%

Source: NCES (2004f)

Figure 4.1

Full-Time Executive/Administrative/Managerial Staff at Public Community Colleges, by Race/Ethnicity: 2002

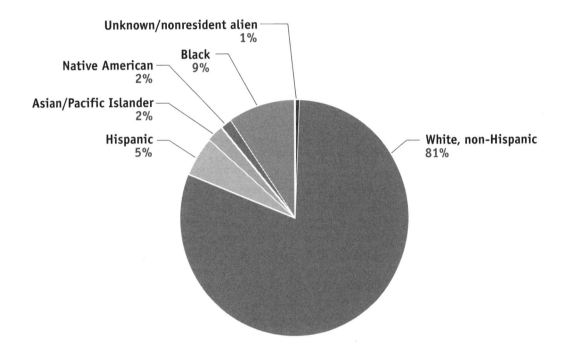

Unknown/nonresident alien 1%

Black 9%

Native American 2%

Asian/Pacific Islander 2%

Hispanic 5%

White, non-Hispanic 81%

Source: NCES (2004f)

Table 4.5

New Full-Time Hires in Public Colleges, by Occupation and Race/Ethnicity: 2001

Occupation	Black	Native American	Asian/ Pacific Islander	Hispanic	Minority subtotal	White	Race/ ethnicity unknown	Non- resident unknown	Total
Community colleges									
Professional staff									
Faculty	500	74	344	422	1,340	6,679	193	83	8,295
Executive/administrative/managerial	114	23	29	72	238	888	21	0	1,147
Other administrative	27	18	6	15	66	269	1	0	336
Other professional (support services)	311	26	79	171	587	1,859	44	19	2,509
Total	952	141	458	680	2,231	9,695	259	102	12,287
Nonprofessional staff									
Technical and paraprofessional	222	47	149	250	668	1,375	56	7	2,106
Clerical and secretarial	493	42	219	473	1,227	2,481	62	8	3,778
Skilled crafts	20	4	8	29	61	166	2	0	229
Service/maintenance	342	31	67	204	644	880	19	1	1,544
Total	1,077	124	443	956	2,600	4,902	139	16	7,657
Total community college staff	2,029	265	901	1,636	4,831	14,597	398	118	19,944
Distribution									
Professional staff									
Faculty	6.0%	0.9%	4.1%	5.1%	16.2%	80.5%	2.3%	1.0%	100.0%
Executive/administrative/managerial	9.9%	2.0%	2.5%	6.3%	20.7%	77.4%	1.8%	0.0%	100.0%
Other administrative	8.0%	5.4%	1.8%	4.5%	19.6%	80.1%	0.3%	0.0%	100.0%
Other professional (support services)	12.4%	1.0%	3.1%	6.8%	23.4%	74.1%	1.8%	0.8%	100.0%
Total	7.7%	1.1%	3.7%	5.5%	18.2%	78.9%	2.1%	0.8%	100.0%
Nonprofessional staff									
Technical and paraprofessional	10.5%	2.2%	7.1%	11.9%	31.7%	65.3%	2.7%	0.3%	100.0%
Clerical and secretarial	13.0%	1.1%	5.8%	12.5%	32.5%	65.7%	1.6%	0.2%	100.0%
Skilled crafts	8.7%	1.7%	3.5%	12.7%	26.6%	72.5%	0.9%	0.0%	100.0%
Service/maintenance	22.2%	2.0%	4.3%	13.2%	41.7%	57.0%	1.2%	0.1%	100.0%
Total	14.1%	1.6%	5.8%	12.5%	34.0%	64.0%	1.8%	0.2%	100.0%
Total community college staff	10.2%	1.3%	4.5%	8.2%	24.2%	73.2%	2.0%	0.6%	100.0%

Occupation	Race/Ethnicity								
	Black	Native American	Asian/ Pacific Islander	Hispanic	Minority subtotal	White	Race/ ethnicity unknown	Non- resident unknown	Total
4-year colleges									
Professional staff									
Faculty	1,569	140	2,108	1,089	4,906	18,236	853	2,644	26,639
Executive/administrative/managerial	387	17	81	89	574	2,140	76	28	2,818
Other administrative	120	10	28	33	191	535	22	23	771
Other professional (support services)	1,948	125	1,515	918	4,506	14,312	558	1,407	20,783
Total	4,024	292	3,732	2,129	10,177	35,223	1,509	4,102	51,011
Nonprofessional staff									
Technical and paraprofessional	799	65	402	435	1,701	3,956	132	187	5,976
Clerical and secretarial	1,896	95	508	1,028	3,527	6,894	264	65	10,750
Skilled crafts	145	13	25	100	283	963	25	2	1,273
Service/maintenance	2,148	48	173	751	3,120	3,015	137	73	6,345
Total	4,988	221	1,108	2,314	8,631	14,828	558	327	24,344
Total 4-year college staff	9,012	513	4,840	4,443	18,808	50,051	2,067	4,429	75,355
Distribution									
Professional staff									
Faculty	5.9%	0.5%	7.9%	4.1%	18.4%	68.5%	3.2%	9.9%	100.0%
Executive/administrative/managerial	13.7%	0.6%	2.9%	3.2%	20.4%	75.9%	2.7%	1.0%	100.0%
Other administrative	15.6%	1.3%	3.6%	4.3%	24.8%	69.4%	2.9%	3.0%	100.0%
Other professional (support services)	9.4%	0.6%	7.3%	4.4%	21.7%	68.9%	2.7%	6.8%	100.0%
Total	7.9%	0.6%	7.3%	4.2%	20.0%	69.0%	3.0%	8.0%	100.0%
Nonprofessional staff									
Technical and paraprofessional	13.4%	1.1%	6.7%	7.3%	28.5%	66.2%	2.2%	3.1%	100.0%
Clerical and secretarial	17.6%	0.9%	4.7%	9.6%	32.8%	64.1%	2.5%	0.6%	100.0%
Skilled crafts	11.4%	1.0%	2.0%	7.9%	22.2%	75.6%	2.0%	0.2%	100.0%
Service/maintenance	33.9%	0.8%	2.7%	11.8%	49.2%	47.5%	2.2%	1.2%	100.0%
Total	20.5%	0.9%	4.6%	9.5%	35.5%	60.9%	2.3%	1.3%	100.0%
Total 4-year college staff	12.0%	0.7%	6.4%	5.9%	25.0%	66.4%	2.7%	5.9%	100.0%

Source: NCES (2004f)

Figure 4.2

New Hires of Full-Time Executive/Administrative/Managerial Staff at Public Community Colleges, by Race/Ethnicity: 2002

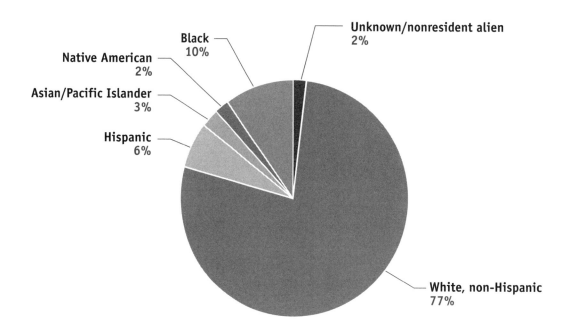

Native American 2%

Black 10%

Asian/Pacific Islander 3%

Hispanic 6%

Unknown/nonresident alien 2%

White, non-Hispanic 77%

Source: NCES (2004f)

Table 4.6
Characteristics of Community College CEOs: 2004

Characteristics	% of All CEOs
Race/ethnicity	
Black	8.5%
Native American	2.8%
Asian/Pacific Islander	1.5%
Hispanic	6.5%
Other	0.5%
Minority subtotal	19.8%
White	80.1%
Gender	
Men	73.5%
Women	26.5%
Age	
under 40	0.5%
40–44	2.5%
45–49	6.8%
50–54	21.5%
55–59	36.9%
60–64	25.2%
65 or older	6.6%
Tenure as a CEO	
0–2.5 years	25.7%
2.6–4 years	21.0%
5–9 years	27.5%
10–14 years	13.9%
15–19 years	6.3%
20–24 years	2.7%
25–29 years	1.6%
30 or more years	1.1%
Highest level of education	
Doctorate (PhD, EdD, etc.)	85.0%
JD	2.0%
Master's	11.0%
Other	1.0%

Source: AACC (2004a); Blount & Associates & Lindley (2005)

Table 4.7
Compensation of Community College CEOs: 2004

College Type	Base Salary		Total Cash Contributions	
	Average	Median	Average	Median
Single-campus college	$126,504	$125,000	$132,109	$130,531
Main campus of a multicampus college	$145,920	$139,000	$152,347	$145,000
College of a multicollege district	$138,144	$136,800	$142,207	$141,530
Campus of a multicampus system	$102,438	$109,491	$107,357	$110,000
2-year campus of a university, separate accreditation	$121,701	$126,700	$125,148	$127,000
District office of a multicollege district	$182,294	$184,291	$193,065	$187,100
2-year campus of a university, sharing accreditation	$114,772	$104,500	$115,858	$104,500

Source: Blount & Associates & Lindley (2005)

Note. Base salary includes salary from the college and, where applicable, the college foundation. Total cash contributions include salary and nonsalary cash contributions provided by the college and, where applicable, the college foundation.

Table 4.8
Employee Benefits Received by Community College CEOs: 2004

Benefits	Coverage			
	100% covered	Partial coverage	Not covered by the college	Not offered by the college
Individual medical coverage				
Medical	49%	49%	1%	0%
Prescription drugs	30%	62%	3%	3%
Dental	30%	47%	18%	3%
Vision	22%	38%	16%	17%
Hearing	11%	28%	7%	40%
Individual insurance coverage				
Life	55%	27%	10%	4%
Long-term disability	36%	21%	23%	13%
Short-term disability	31%	17%	22%	19%
Accidental death and dismemberment	31%	16%	20%	22%
Travel accident	13%	3%	9%	60%
Long-term care	6%	6%	27%	45%
Family coverage				
Medical	24%	50%	20%	3%
Prescription drugs	16%	55%	20%	6%
Dental	17%	43%	29%	6%
Vision	13%	33%	23%	21%
Hearing	7%	25%	12%	39%
Life	4%	10%	26%	44%

Source: Blount & Associates & Lindley (2005)

Table 4.9

College Faculty, by Age and Employment Status: 1998–1999

Employment Status and Type of College/Program	Age					
	Under 35	35–44	45–54	55–64	65–69	70+
Employed full time						
Public 4-year, with doctoral programs	7.4%	27.7%	34.4%	24.2%	4.8%	1.4%
Private nonprofit 4-year, with doctoral programs	8.3%	28.7%	33.7%	22.9%	4.7%	1.6%
Public 4-year, no doctoral programs	6.6%	21.6%	34.8%	30.9%	4.8%	1.3%
Private nonprofit 4-year, no doctoral programs	7.6%	26.4%	36.3%	24.8%	3.5%	1.5%
Public community college	6.5%	21.9%	41.2%	27.1%	2.2%	1.0%
Private nonprofit community college	15.8%	12.8%	32.1%	28.9%	8.0%	2.3%
Total	7.3%	25.3%	36.0%	25.9%	4.1%	1.4%
Employed part time						
Public 4-year, with doctoral programs	13.6%	28.8%	28.8%	17.9%	7.7%	3.1%
Private nonprofit 4-year, with doctoral programs	7.5%	27.1%	29.3%	19.9%	4.8%	11.5%
Public 4-year, no doctoral programs	12.7%	21.8%	36.8%	19.6%	4.4%	4.7%
Private nonprofit 4-year, no doctoral programs	14.8%	25.7%	32.0%	16.4%	6.3%	4.7%
Public community college	12.1%	25.8%	37.3%	18.2%	4.3%	2.2%
Private nonprofit community college	8.0%	30.7%	29.6%	25.3%	4.3%	2.1%
Total	12.6%	25.9%	34.1%	18.2%	5.3%	3.9%

Source: NCES (2004k)

Figure 4.3

Full-Time Faculty's Years to Retirement, by College Type: 1999–2000

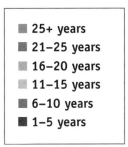

- 25+ years
- 21–25 years
- 16–20 years
- 11–15 years
- 6–10 years
- 1–5 years

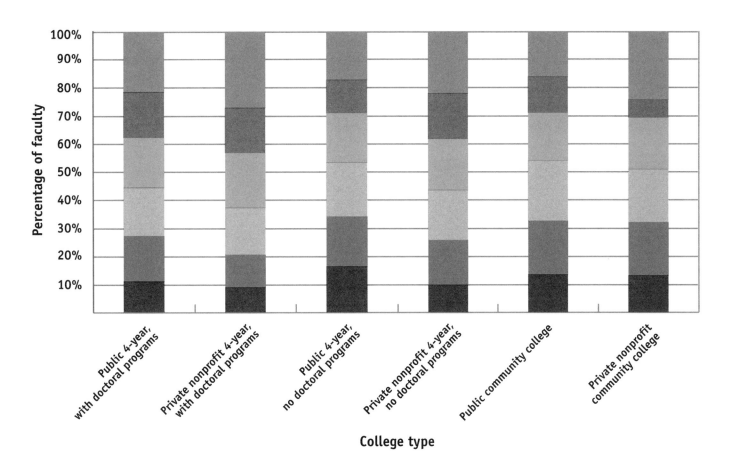

Source: NCES (2004k)

Table 4.10

Highest Level of Education Attained by College Faculty, by Employment Status and Teaching Field: 1998–1999

Employment Status and Type of College/Teaching Field	Highest Level of Education					
	Doctorate	First professional	Master's	Bachelor's	Associate	Less than associate degree
Employed full time						
Public 4-year, with doctoral programs	70.1%	14.1%	13.9%	1.7%	0.0%	0.1%
Private nonprofit 4-year, with doctoral programs	66.7%	23.6%	8.1%	1.5%	0.1%	0.1%
Public 4-year, no doctoral programs	69.4%	2.1%	26.2%	2.2%	0.0%	0.2%
Private nonprofit 4-year, no doctoral programs	59.1%	6.0%	32.2%	2.3%	0.1%	0.3%
Private nonprofit community college	18.2%	1.9%	61.7%	12.7%	3.4%	2.1%
Public community college	20.3%	2.3%	58.3%	17.8%	0.0%	1.4%
Business, law, and communications	8.6%	6.8%	68.2%	14.1%	0.7%	1.6%
Health sciences	4.5%	2.4%	62.0%	22.5%	6.8%	1.7%
Humanities	29.8%	0.9%	68.3%	0.8%	0.3%	0.0%
Natural sciences and engineering	25.5%	1.3%	57.0%	12.9%	2.9%	0.4%
Social sciences and education	26.6%	1.7%	67.9%	3.1%	0.7%	0.0%
Occupation-specific programs	10.0%	0.9%	33.6%	31.1%	11.9%	12.5%
All other programs	11.1%	0.4%	67.3%	13.6%	4.1%	3.5%
Total full time	57.7%	9.2%	27.8%	4.0%	0.7%	0.2%
Employed part time						
Public 4-year, with doctoral programs	28.8%	21.5%	42.0%	7.1%	0.3%	0.3%
Private nonprofit 4-year, with doctoral programs	35.4%	18.4%	36.0%	9.9%	0.2%	0.1%
Public 4-year, no doctoral programs	21.2%	6.1%	60.6%	11.2%	0.2%	0.7%
Private nonprofit 4-year, no doctoral programs	22.6%	9.7%	55.6%	11.1%	0.2%	0.8%
Private nonprofit community college	8.2%	2.7%	58.6%	19.8%	5.6%	5.2%
Public community college	7.9%	4.8%	64.1%	21.1%	2.1%	0.0%
Business, law, and communications	2.4%	8.1%	56.4%	25.6%	4.7%	3.0%
Health sciences	2.4%	3.5%	40.5%	31.6%	13.2%	8.8%
Humanities	12.6%	1.3%	76.1%	9.8%	0.0%	0.3%
Natural sciences and engineering	9.8%	2.0%	61.5%	19.2%	4.6%	2.9%
Social sciences and education	14.2%	2.7%	69.5%	12.6%	1.0%	0.0%
Occupationally specific programs	4.5%	2.7%	16.3%	24.5%	25.1%	26.8%
All other programs	3.0%	0.7%	57.7%	28.3%	5.8%	4.6%
Total part time	18.2%	8.7%	54.1%	14.1%	2.5%	1.1%

Source: NCES (2004k)

Table 4.11

Time Spent on Activities by Full-Time College Faculty: 1998–1999

Type of College/Program	Faculty's Activities			
	Teaching	Research	Administration	All other activities
Public 4-year, with doctoral programs	46.4%	24.0%	13.7%	16.0%
Private nonprofit 4-year, with doctoral programs	43.4%	25.9%	14.1%	16.6%
Public 4-year, no doctoral programs	63.2%	10.5%	13.4%	13.0%
Private nonprofit 4-year, no doctoral programs	62.4%	8.3%	16.7%	12.5%
Public community college	71.9%	3.8%	11.5%	12.9%
Private nonprofit community college	61.3%	4.5%	20.2%	14.0%
Total	56.7%	15.2%	13.9%	14.3%

Source: NCES (2004k)

Table 4.12

Percentage of Community Colleges Offering International Programs and Services: 1995 and 2000

Program	% of Colleges	
	1995	**2000**
Global awareness activities	43%	83%
International business activities	23%	60%
International components in classes	40%	82%

Source: Blair, Phinney, & Phillippe (2001)

Table 4.13

Top 30 Community Colleges, by Nonresident Alien Student Enrollment: 2002

College	City	State	# enrolled
Houston Community College System	Houston	TX	3,970
Santa Monica College	Santa Monica	CA	2,755
Broward Community College	Fort Lauderdale	FL	2,525
Borough of Manhattan Community College	New York	NY	2,102
Collin County Community College District	Plano	TX	1,893
Miami Dade College	Miami	FL	1,888
Montgomery College Central Administration	Rockville	MD	1,854
LaGuardia Community College	Long Island City	NY	1,561
Northern Virginia Community College	Annandale	VA	1,532
Oakland Community College	Bloomfield Hills	MI	1,328
Central Piedmont Community College	Charlotte	NC	1,288
City College of San Francisco	San Francisco	CA	1,197
De Anza College	Cupertino	CA	1,168
Richland College	Dallas	TX	1,091
Nassau Community College	Garden City	NY	1,040
Pasadena City College	Pasadena	CA	1,027
Foothill College	Los Altos Hills	CA	1,000
Bergen Community College	Paramus	NJ	949
Valencia Community College	Orlando	FL	922
Wake Technical Community College	Raleigh	NC	905
Georgia Perimeter College	Decatur	GA	824
Moraine Valley Community College	Palos Hills	IL	808
North Harris Montgomery Community College District	The Woodlands	TX	793
Oklahoma City Community College	Oklahoma City	OK	788
Quincy College	Quincy	MA	752
Grossmont College	El Cajon	CA	749
El Camino College	Torrance	CA	744
Palm Beach Community College	Lake Worth	FL	728
Diablo Valley College	Pleasant Hill	CA	721
Kingsborough Community College	Brooklyn	NY	717

Source: Blair, Phinney, & Phillippe (2001)

Table 4.14

Percentage of Colleges Offering Certificate- or Degree-Level Distance Education Programs, by College Type and Size: 2000–2001

College Type and Size	Offered any distance education courses	Any college-level certificate or degree programs		Programs Designed to Be Completed Entirely Through Distance Education					
				Certificate programs			Degree programs		
		All colleges	Colleges with distance education programs	Certificate programs at either level	Under-graduate certificate programs	Graduate/ first-professional certificate programs	Degree programs at either level	Under-graduate degree programs	Graduate/ first-professional degree programs
College type									
Public community college	90%	22%	25%	15%	15%	—	20%	20%	—
Public 4-year college	89%	47%	53%	25%	13%	18%	48%	28%	43%
Private 4-year college	40%	14%	36%	14%	10%	10%	33%	19%	28%
Size of college									
Less than 3,000 students	41%	11%	27%	12%	11%	6%	22%	16%	21%
3,000–9,999 students	88%	32%	37%	14%	12%	12%	34%	25%	38%
10,000 or more students	95%	49%	51%	30%	16%	30%	47%	27%	57%
All colleges	56%	19%	34%	16%	12%	13%	30%	21%	35%

Source: NCES (2004e)

Note. Percentages are based on the estimated 4,130 community and 4-year Title IV-eligible, degree-granting colleges in the nation. Detail may not sum to totals because of rounding.

Table 4.15

Number and Percentage Distribution of 2-Year and 4-Year Title IV Degree-Granting Colleges, by Distance Education Program Status: 2000–2001

College Type and Size	Total # of colleges	Distance Education Program Status					
		Offered in 2000–2001		Planned to offer in the next 3 years		Did not offer in 2000–2001, did not plan to offer in the next 3 years	
		#	%	#	%	#	%
College type							
Public community college	1,070	960	90%	50	5%	50	5%
Private community college	640	100	16%	150	23%	400	62%
Public 4-year college	620	550	89%	20	3%	50	8%
Private 4-year college	1,800	710	40%	290	16%	790	44%
Size of college							
Less than 3,000 students	2,840	1,160	41%	460	16%	1,220	43%
3,000–9,999 students	870	770	88%	50	5%	60	7%
10,000 or more students	420	400	95%	10	2%	10	2%
All colleges	4,130	2,320	56%	510	12%	1,290	31%

Source: Waits & Lewis (2003)

Note. Percentages are based on the estimated 4,130 community and 4-year Title IV-eligible, degree-granting colleges in the nation. Detail may not sum to totals because of rounding.

Figure 4.4

Enrollment in Distance Education Courses, by Type of College: 2000–2001

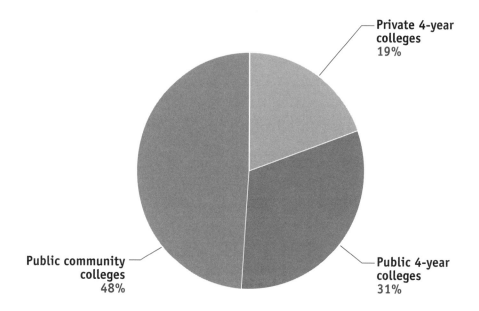

Private 4-year colleges
19%

Public 4-year colleges
31%

Public community colleges
48%

Source: Waits & Lewis (2003)

Figure 4.5
Community Colleges Offering Service Learning: 2003

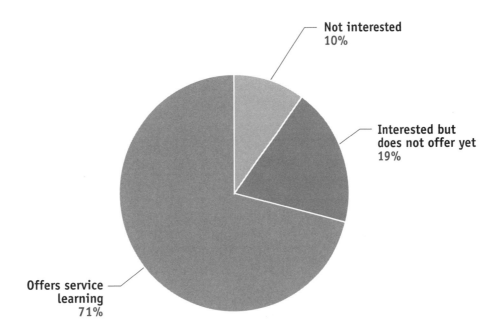

Not interested
10%

Interested but
does not offer yet
19%

Offers service
learning
71%

Source: Prentice, Robinson, & McPhee (2003)

Figure 4.6

Curricular Areas in Which Community Colleges Offer Service Learning Activities: 2003

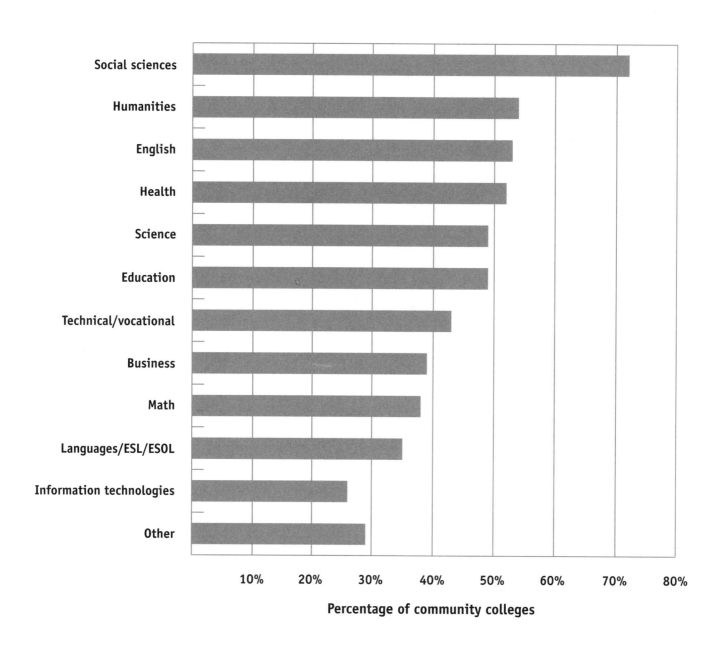

Source: Prentice, Robinson, & McPhee (2003)

V

College Education Costs and Financing

Americans continue to believe that a college education is essential for economic success and civic participation, according to recent *Chronicle of Higher Education* survey reports (Selingo, 2003, 2004). They favor universal access and have considerable confidence in colleges and universities to provide high-quality learning experiences. Nevertheless, nearly 80% of middle-class respondents in the survey worried that they would have difficulty funding college studies for their children or themselves. These are legitimate worries: Between 1991–1992 and 2001–2002 tuition at all colleges rose by 74%, and for community colleges, tuition increased from an average of $1,189 in 1991–1992 to $1,772 in 2001–2002, an increase of about 49% (see Table 5.5).

The costs of attending community colleges are still favorable when contrasted with an average cost in 2002 of $10,636 for tuition, room, and board at public four-year colleges and $26,854 at private four-

year colleges. These tuition and fee levels and their annual rate of growth differ considerably depending on the region of the country. Furthermore, at public community colleges and four-year colleges alike, these costs have tended to rise more rapidly in recent years because of lower levels of state and local appropriations for higher education.

Many students try to offset college costs through federal and state grants and loans. In 2002–2003, more than $40 billion was distributed nationwide to eligible students by federal and state governments and colleges and universities. Approximately one third of Pell dollars (about $4.4 billion in 2003) was awarded to community college students. The annual grant aid maximum was $4,050 per student, but awards averaged $2,000, which generally covered the entire tuition amount.

Still, students had to cover other education-related costs, such as those for books, child care, and transportation, and continued to feel financial

stress as a result. Many had to work part or full time to support their studies, and this sometimes had a negative impact on their academic progress. Changes in government policies, generally at the state level, have also affected the distribution of financial aid grants, providing proportionally more dollars for meritorious middle-class students and fewer dollars for needy low-income students. Finally, there has been a shift away from grants that need not be repaid (42% of awards in 2000) and toward loans that may leave students with heavy debts upon graduation. In 2000, only 42% of financial aid awards were grants, whereas 58% were loans (Lane, 2003).

In spite of this grim outlook for college costs, enrollments in all economic, racial, and ethnic groups have grown since the 1980s, and community colleges strive to stay true to their open-door policy, providing access for many who otherwise could not attend college. However, severe funding cuts in several states, including California and

Florida, have resulted in faculty and staff hiring freezes. Because of the surge in enrollments in these states, when classes filled, additional classes could not always be opened to accommodate all the potential students, and late registrants were actually turned away. Officials in California estimated that close to 175,000 students were turned away from community colleges in 2003–2004; in North Carolina, some 56,000 students were not able to register (Evelyn, 2004).

At the same time that students and their families are trying to find affordable higher education options, community colleges are working hard to contain and even reduce costs while maintaining a full range of services and programs. Generally community college revenues, which nationwide approach $33 billion annually (see Table 5.1) are derived from the following sources: tuition and fees; federal, state, and local funds; and grants, gifts, and sales. The proportion from each source depends on the college's location, with state funding usually playing the pivotal role. Although on the average, public community colleges receive approximately equal revenue from state, local, and tuition dollars, the total amount of support colleges receive varies greatly, with very few states actually receiving one third of their revenues from each. In fact,

states such as Kansas, Illinois, and Arizona receive a larger portion of their total revenue from local sources than from the state. Other states, such as Florida, Indiana, and Massachusetts, receive more than 50% of their revenue from the state. Still others, including New Hampshire, Vermont, and Pennsylvania, depend more heavily on tuition than do either of the other two revenue streams.

Perhaps the greatest challenge for community colleges in the near future will be maintaining current service levels in light of their states' fiscal difficulties. In effect, states will have to increase funding for higher education by 5%–6% annually just to maintain the status quo while also accounting for inflation, expected high school graduation rates, and consequent college enrollment increases. However, the majority of states—particularly those that rely on sales taxes rather than property taxes for revenue—have a structural deficit of 0.5% annually in funding current services. That is, these states would have to increase taxes by 0.5% each year just to fund the services that are currently supported. Alternatively, the states would have to hold spending growth to about 4.5% annually rather than the 5% needed to maintain current services.

This built-in problem was less noticeable in good economic times,

but the past few years have been characterized by slow growth and recession. In such times, the general public is less willing or able to spend, thus reducing sales tax revenues. At the same time, legislators are highly resistant to raising taxes. The situation is further complicated by the public demand for increased services in other areas, such as K–12 education, prisons, and health care. These other services are viewed as necessities, whereas higher education is sometimes seen as a luxury that is less deserving of public funding.

Whatever the economic distress of states in the past few years, they are still major contributors to community college finances, and most have developed elaborate means for deciding how much to allocate to the colleges. A survey conducted in 2000 by the Denver-based Education Commission of the States Community College Policy Center revealed that 29 states used a funding formula to determine appropriations, whereas 15 states did not do so. Elements in these formulas may include enrollment in current and past years, enrollment projections, space utilization, and comparison with peer colleges. Because workplace training has become so critical to the economic vitality of communities, some states are also beginning to reimburse colleges for noncredit workplace training courses. This is a significant change from as recent as a decade ago when noncredit courses were largely recreational in nature or provided a forum for learning new hobbies.

In recent years, many states have also introduced performance-based initiatives to allocate some proportion of the funds as a means of holding colleges and universities accountable and ensuring that taxpayer dollars spent on higher education benefit the state optimally. Ten states reported that performance on designated indicators was tied directly to budget allocations. Some of the most frequently used performance indicators were job placement, transfer rates, graduation rates, retention, pass rates on licensure examinations, and student satisfaction surveys.

Containing tuition costs becomes increasingly difficult as funding has shifted from the federal government to states and, in some cases, from states to local sources. In virtually all states, these shifts have affected tuition. To illustrate this shift, between 1980 and 1996 federal appropriations for community colleges declined by 69%, and state appropriations grew by only 7%. In that same period, tuition and fees increased by 117%, and local appropriations (county or municipality) grew by 47%. To keep tuition costs from rising even higher, most colleges have tapped other revenue sources to compensate for the loss of public funds, including grants, private donations, and auxiliary services income such as that from cafeterias, bookstores, and vending machines.

Some colleges are able to charge special rates for customized training and do sufficient training of this type to help support other programs or needs at the college. Other colleges establish close partnerships with local businesses to share education or training costs. An example of this practice is a partnership between a college and a local hospital in which the hospital in need of qualified nursing staff provides classroom and clinical lab space and funds some of the faculty to teach specific courses for the associate degree nursing program. The relationship may include tuition grants to students that will be waived in exchange for the student working at the college for a specified period of time after graduation. This trend has led to observations that public higher education is becoming privatized.

Operating expenditures for community colleges are categorized largely as follows: instruction, academic support (library, tutoring, etc.), student services, public/community services, administrative costs, physical plant operation and maintenance, and scholarships. Between 1980 and 1996, these expenditures increased by 49% in constant dollars, with scholarships growing by 660%, perhaps to reduce the impact of tuition increases on students (Merisotis & Wolanin, 2000).

It is important to note that, in the service-intensive field of education, personnel costs account for approximately 85% of the budget. Colleges have attempted to keep these costs low by hiring greater numbers of part-time staff and adjunct instructors and by not filling some positions. Because cuts in full-time personnel often involve contracts and tenure issues, colleges have generally avoided this strategy for reducing costs, choosing instead to increase class sizes, encourage early retirements, and delay equipment purchases, among other measures. The pressure to keep budgets from expanding has had to be balanced against demands for new programs and additional support services such as career counseling, job placement, and online student services. The rising price of utilities, health benefits, and technology, together with the need to address problems resulting from deferred maintenance of aging physical plants, has put even more stress on their budgets.

In the view of some legislators and members of the public, higher education has operated inefficiently for many years because the cost of attending college has increased at a faster rate than has the cost of living.

Yet introducing cost-effectiveness strategies and tightening the fiscal belt have neither reduced college costs nor changed negative public perceptions appreciably. To counteract this view, community colleges have developed sophisticated economic models to demonstrate the value of their contributions to local and state economies. They have also become more entrepreneurial, diversifying their revenue streams through partnerships with business and industry, sale of assets such as real estate, and customized training programs that may supply the college with state-of-the-art equipment.

Distance learning is another means colleges have used in the attempt to contain costs and enhance revenues. Providing courses online has allowed colleges to reach underserved populations and accommodate workers who want to learn whenever they can and wherever they are. This strategy has resulted in new enrollments and additional tuition income, while not straining physical facilities where space is at a premium. However, the expectation that offering degrees and courses online could be done at a lower cost than on campus has not proved true. When the cost of faculty training, high-tech equipment, and round-the-clock technical support is taken into account, distance education may actually increase costs.

Fundraising is yet another means to supplement funding allocations. The first two-year college foundation was established sometime in the 1920s at Long Beach City College in California, and since that time these ancillary organizations have assumed a significant role in supporting college programs and services. According to a 1997 survey by AACC, 88% of responding community colleges had a foundation, with average assets estimated at over $2 million (Phillippe & Eblinger, 1998). Through the contributions of businesses, alumni, friends of the college, and foundation board members, these foundations raise money for scholarships, equipment purchases, facilities improvements, and many other college needs.

As fiscal support from public sources has dwindled, community college foundations have evolved into highly sophisticated operations that manage large investments, conduct capital campaigns, and link with alumni services. Annual solicitations, golf tournaments, social events, and planned giving programs are other foundation activities on behalf of their colleges. Furthermore, just as at four-year colleges, fundraising has become a primary function of community college presidents (up to 40% of their time), and many colleges have added development offices to support this crucial work.

In their second century of existence, community colleges will have to address these and other financial conditions as they compete in a globalized education environment. Ever-increasing costs for personnel and institutional operations, surging enrollments, competition from other education providers, evolving workforce development needs, and new technologies will all require creative responses and new funding approaches. The continued diversification of the student body and the influx of immigrants will lead to new or expanded needs for targeted support services. Remedial education will continue to be an important component of the colleges' programming in order to ensure students' success. Demands for accountability and cost effectiveness will not disappear. Still, community colleges have proven over the past 100 years that they are capable of meeting such challenges, and they can be expected to continue using all resources optimally to prepare students for successful roles in American society. ⊕

Figure 5.1
Sources of Revenue for Public Colleges: 2001–2002

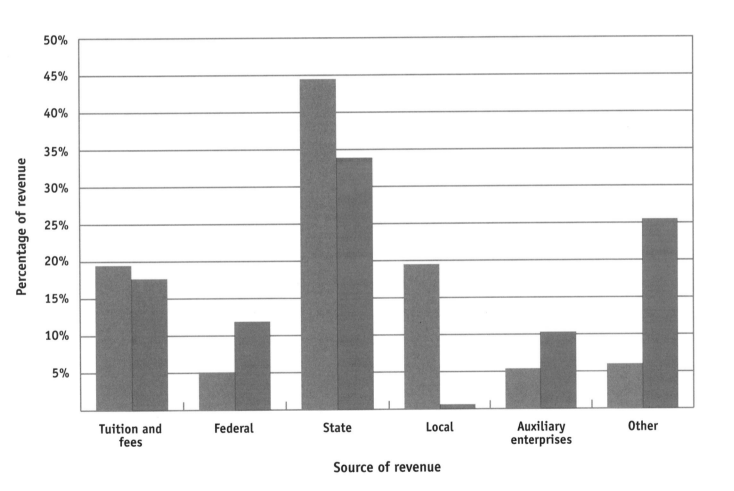

Source: Knapp et al. (2004); NCES (2004g)

Note. Includes only colleges that use the Government Accounting Standards Board accounting standards.

Table 5.1

Sources of Revenue for Colleges: 2000–2001

College Type and Source of Funds	Community Colleges Revenues ($1,000s)	%	4-Year Colleges Revenues ($1,000s)	%
Public colleges (GASB)[a]				
Tuition and fees	$6,133,203	19.5%	$25,330,908	17.7%
Government appropriations	$17,249,414	54.9%	$45,984,845	32.1%
Federal	$77,304	0.2%	$1,638,648	1.1%
State	$11,831,392	37.6%	$44,117,490	30.8%
Local	$5,340,718	17.0%	$228,707	0.2%
Government grants and contracts	$4,457,986	14.2%	$20,554,713	14.4%
Federal (excluding Pell grants)	$1,524,435	4.8%	$15,427,544	10.8%
State	$2,150,460	6.8%	$4,443,486	3.1%
Local	$783,092	2.5%	$683,683	0.5%
Private gifts, grants, and contracts	$376,197	1.2%	$8,464,323	5.9%
Endowment income	$27,617	0.1%	$1,247,897	0.9%
Sales and services of educational activities	$228,442	0.7%	$4,749,548	3.3%
Auxiliary enterprises	$1,696,626	5.4%	$14,682,143	10.3%
Hospitals	$0	0.0%	$15,936,422	11.1%
Independent operations	$134,853	0.4%	$801,778	0.6%
Other sources	$1,134,545	3.6%	$5,311,191	3.7%
Total current funds revenues	$31,438,882	100.0%	$143,063,768	100.0%
Public colleges (FASB)[b]				
Tuition and fees	$1,731	7.1%	$453,770	21.4%
Government appropriations	$16,066	66.3%	$320,915	15.1%
Federal	$14	0.1%	$3,997	0.2%
State	$3,190	13.2%	$316,918	15.0%
Local	$12,863	53.1%	$0	0.0%
Government grants and contracts	$4,634	19.1%	$168,044	7.9%
Federal (excluding Pell grants)	$4,080	16.8%	$132,273	6.2%
State	$500	2.1%	$32,457	1.5%
Local	$54	0.2%	$3,315	0.2%
Private gifts, grants, and contracts	$289	1.2%	$107,513	5.1%
Contributions from affiliated entities	$0	0.0%	$0	0.0%
Investment returns	$180	0.7%	$76,294	3.6%
Sales and services of educational activities	$0	0.0%	$10,383	0.5%
Sales and services of auxiliary enterprises	$1,158	4.8%	$121,908	5.8%
Hospitals	$0	0.0%	$823,499	38.9%
Independent operations	$41	0.2%	$0	0.0%
Other revenue	$138	0.6%	$36,002	1.7%
Total revenues and investment returns	$24,237	100.0%	$2,118,328	100.0%

College Type and Source of Funds	Community Colleges		4-Year Colleges	
	Revenues ($1,000s)	%	Revenues ($1,000s)	%
Private nonprofit colleges				
Tuition and fees	$321,724	53.1%	$30,996,381	38.0%
Government appropriations	$8,912	1.5%	$770,523	0.9%
Federal	$3,712	0.6%	$374,051	0.5%
State	$4,870	0.8%	$382,486	0.5%
Local	$329	0.1%	$13,986	0.0%
Government grants and contracts	$73,435	12.1%	$10,708,529	13.1%
Federal (excluding Pell grants)	$53,714	8.9%	$9,445,497	11.6%
State	$14,687	2.4%	$774,017	0.9%
Local	$5,034	0.8%	$489,016	0.6%
Private gifts, grants, and contracts	$58,617	9.7%	$14,978,461	18.4%
Contributions from affiliated entities	$11,827	2.0%	$810,408	1.0%
Investment returns	$20,996	3.5%	-$3,623,323	-4.4%
Sales and services of educational activities	$15,949	2.6%	$3,452,731	4.2%
Sales and services of auxiliary enterprises	$39,294	6.5%	$8,703,316	10.7%
Hospitals	$694	0.1%	$7,125,648	8.7%
Independent operations	$2,020	0.3%	$3,499,024	4.3%
Other revenue	$52,096	8.6%	$4,147,227	5.1%
Total revenues and investment returns	$605,564	100.0%	$81,568,928	100.0%
Private for-profit colleges				
Tuition and fees	$1,756,833	87.2%	$2,583,644	87.5%
Government appropriations, grants, and contracts	$132,901	6.6%	$141,801	4.8%
Federal (excluding Pell grants)	$105,474	5.2%	$81,879	2.8%
State and local	$27,426	1.4%	$59,922	2.0%
Private grants and contracts	$1,189	0.1%	$1,659	0.1%
Investment income and gains (losses)	$7,163	0.4%	$12,574	0.4%
Sales and services of educational activities	$23,311	1.2%	$40,081	1.4%
Sales and services of auxiliary enterprises	$66,660	3.3%	$106,327	3.6%
Other revenue	$27,389	1.4%	$66,168	2.2%
Total revenues and investment returns	$2,015,446	100.0%	$2,952,254	100.0%

Source: Knapp et al. (2004); NCES (2004g)

Note. Public and private colleges use different accounting standards, thus the categories differ. Data are based on the U.S. Department of Education definition of community colleges (see Glossary).

[a]Public colleges that use the Government Accounting Standards Board standards.
[b]Public colleges that use the Financial Accounting Standards Board standards.

Table 5.2

Sources of Expenses for Colleges: 2000–2001

College Type and Source of Funds	Community Colleges Revenues ($1,000s)	%	4-Year Colleges Revenues ($1,000s)	%
Public colleges (GASB)[a]				
Educational and general expenses and transfers[b]	$27,929,494	93.9%	$107,619,308	77.7%
Instruction[b]	$12,891,414	43.3%	$38,387,046	27.7%
Research	$19,889	0.1%	$17,894,529	12.9%
Public service	$726,898	2.4%	$7,600,822	5.5%
Academic support	$2,513,924	8.5%	$10,672,817	7.7%
Student services	$2,993,737	10.1%	$5,315,732	3.8%
Institutional support	$4,517,063	15.2%	$10,703,012	7.7%
Operation and maintenance of plant	$2,799,281	9.4%	$8,174,309	5.9%
Scholarships and fellowships	$1,177,982	4.0%	$6,574,492	4.7%
Mandatory transfers	$289,308	1.0%	$2,296,550	1.7%
Auxiliary enterprises	$1,720,056	5.8%	$14,524,986	10.5%
Hospitals	$0	0.0%	$15,316,448	11.1%
Independent operations	$45,431	0.2%	$732,392	0.5%
Other expenses	$47,486	0.2%	$359,959	0.3%
Total current funds expenses and transfers	$29,742,468	100.0%	$138,553,094	100.0%
Public colleges (FASB)[c]				
Instruction	$7,148	29.8%	$538,801	26.6%
Research	$77	0.3%	$117,330	5.8%
Public service	$285	1.2%	$53,256	2.6%
Academic support	$3,009	12.6%	$138,294	6.8%
Student services	$3,183	13.3%	$64,374	3.2%
Institutional support	$4,900	20.4%	$119,546	5.9%
Auxiliary enterprises	$1,907	8.0%	$130,130	6.4%
Net grant aid to students	$1,292	5.4%	$12,441	0.6%
Hospitals	$0	0.0%	$829,953	41.0%
Independent operations	$1,401	5.8%	$18	0.0%
Other expenses	$770	3.2%	$21,163	1.0%
Total expenses	$23,971	100.0%	$2,025,307	100.0%

College Type and Source of Funds	Community Colleges		4-Year Colleges	
	Revenues ($1,000s)	%	Revenues ($1,000s)	%
Private nonprofit colleges				
Instruction	$193,428	33.5%	$27,413,897	32.2%
Research	$5,772	1.0%	$9,019,966	10.6%
Public service	$5,967	1.0%	$1,467,325	1.7%
Academic support	$34,412	6.0%	$7,333,851	8.6%
Student services	$80,717	14.0%	$6,036,478	7.1%
Institutional support	$141,764	24.6%	$11,292,310	13.3%
Auxiliary enterprises	$52,880	9.2%	$8,957,973	10.5%
Net grant aid to students	$15,500	2.7%	$1,160,660	1.4%
Hospitals	$1,896	0.3%	$7,253,479	8.5%
Independent operations	$1,510	0.3%	$3,133,099	3.7%
Other expenses	$43,046	7.5%	$1,979,086	2.3%
Total expenses	$576,893	100.0%	$85,048,123	100.0%
Private for-profit colleges				
Instruction	$583,727	32.1%	$726,328	30.1%
Research and public service	$18,019	1.0%	$4,878	0.2%
Academic support, student services, and institutional support	$952,056	52.3%	$1,385,095	57.4%
Auxiliary enterprises	$67,872	3.7%	$113,371	4.7%
Net grant aid to students	$25,269	1.4%	$18,519	0.8%
Other expenses	$174,184	9.6%	$166,465	6.9%
Total expenses	$1,821,126	100.0%	$2,414,655	100.0%

Source: Knapp et al. (2004); NCES (2004g)

Note. Data are based on the U.S. Department of Education definition of community colleges (see Glossary).

[a]Public colleges that use the Government Accounting Standards Board standards.

[a]Excludes Pell Grants and nonmandatory transfers.

[c]Public colleges that use the Financial Accounting Standards Board standards.

Figure 5.2
Sources of Expenses for Public Colleges: 2001–2002

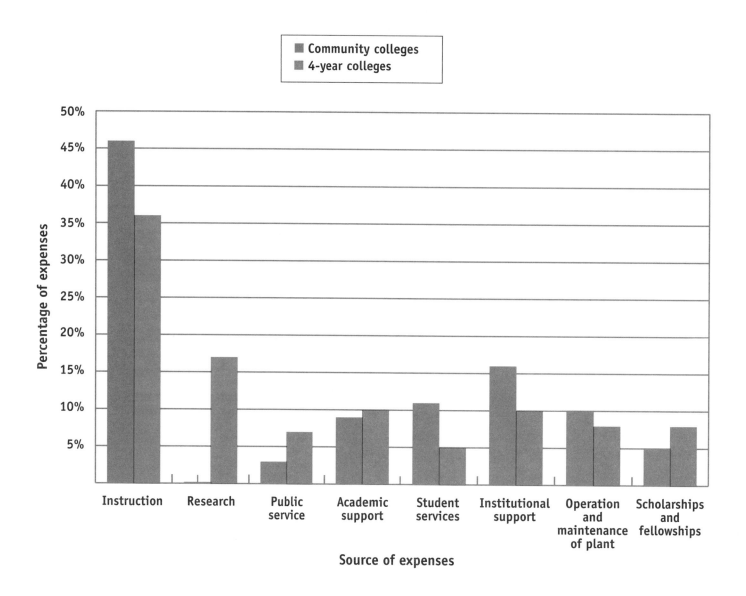

Source: Knapp et al. (2004); NCES (2004g)

Note. Data pertain only to colleges that use the Government Accounting Standards Board accounting standards.

American Association of Community Colleges

Table 5.3

Sources of Scholarship and Fellowship Funds for Colleges: 2000–2001

College Type and Source of Funds	Community Colleges		4-Year Colleges	
	Revenues ($1,000s)	%	Revenues ($1,000s)	%
Public colleges (GASB)[a]				
Federal government	$2,687,724	73.3%	$3,462,540	36.6%
Pell grants	$2,489,909	67.9%	$2,894,741	30.6%
Other federal grants	$197,815	5.4%	$567,799	6.0%
State government	$605,393	16.5%	$2,252,641	23.8%
Local government	$12,059	0.3%	$10,323	0.1%
Private	$104,595	2.9%	$941,725	9.9%
Institutional	$258,121	7.0%	$2,802,004	29.6%
Total scholarships and fellowships	$3,667,891	100.0%	$9,469,233	100.0%
Public colleges (FASB)[b]				
Federal government	$968	60.5%	$29,397	25.2%
Pell grants	$689	43.1%	$23,836	20.4%
Other federal grants	$279	17.5%	$5,561	4.8%
State government	$128	8.0%	$14,896	12.8%
Local government	$232	14.5%	$0	0.0%
Private	$270	16.9%	$10,080	8.6%
Institutional	$0	0.0%	$62,293	53.4%
Total scholarships and fellowships	$1,599	100.0%	$116,665	100.0%
Private nonprofit colleges				
Federal government	$57,694	45.7%	$1,874,848	14.1%
Pell grants	$50,182	39.7%	$1,118,502	8.4%
Other federal grants	$7,512	6.0%	$756,345	5.7%
State government	$36,127	28.6%	$1,258,774	9.4%
Local government	$2,136	1.7%	$50,508	0.4%
Private	$13,753	10.9%	$2,565,327	19.2%
Institutional	$16,536	13.1%	$7,586,944	56.9%
Total scholarships and fellowships	$126,246	100.0%	$13,336,401	100.0%
Private for-profit colleges				
Federal government	$387,241	74.1%	$268,739	62.6%
Pell grants	$309,159	59.1%	$228,423	53.2%
Other federal grants	$78,082	14.9%	$40,316	9.4%
State and local grants	$123,150	23.6%	$126,330	29.4%
Institutional	$12,341	2.4%	$34,226	8.0%
Total scholarships and fellowships	$522,731	100.0%	$429,296	100.0%

Source: Knapp et al. (2004); NCES (2004g)

Note. Data are based on the U.S. Department of Education definition of community colleges (see Glossary).

[a]Public colleges that use the Government Accounting Standards Board standards.

[b]Public colleges that use Financial Accounting Standards Board standards.

Table 5.4

College Tuition and Fee Revenues and Federal Grant Scholarship Expenses: 2000–2001

Revenues and Grant Expenses by College Type	Community Colleges		4-Year Colleges	
	Amount ($1,000s)	% of tuition and fee revenue	Amount ($1,000s)	% of tuition and fee revenue
Public colleges (GASB)[a]				
Tuition and fee revenue	$6,133,203		$25,330,908	
Pell grant funds spent	$2,489,909	40.6%	$2,894,741	11.4%
Other federal grant funds spent	$197,815	3.2%	$567,799	2.2%
Total federal funds spent	$2,687,724	43.8%	$3,462,540	13.7%
Public colleges (FASB)[b]				
Tuition and fee revenue	$1,731		$453,770	
Pell grant funds spent	$689	39.8%	$23,836	5.3%
Other federal grant funds spent	$279	16.1%	$5,561	1.2%
Total federal funds spent	$968	55.9%	$29,397	6.5%
Private nonprofit colleges				
Tuition and fee revenue	$321,724		$30,996,381	
Pell grant funds spent	$50,182	15.6%	$1,118,502	3.6%
Other federal grant funds spent	$7,512	2.3%	$756,345	2.4%
Total federal funds spent	$57,694	17.9%	$1,874,847	6.0%
Private for-profit colleges				
Tuition and fee revenue	$1,756,833		$2,583,644	
Pell grant funds spent	$309,159	17.6%	$228,423	8.8%
Other federal grant funds spent	$78,082	4.4%	$40,316	1.6%
Total federal funds spent	$387,241	22.0%	$268,739	10.4%

Source: Knapp et al. (2004); NCES (2004g)

[a]Public colleges that use the Government Accounting Standards Board standards.
[b]Public colleges that use Financial Accounting Standards Board standards.

Table 5.5

Average College Tuition and Fees: 1976–2002
(in current dollars)

Academic Year	Community Colleges			4-Year Colleges			All Colleges		
	Public	Independent	Total	Public	Independent	Total	Public	Independent	Total
1976–1977	$283	$1,592	$346	$617	$2,534	$1,218	$479	$2,467	$924
1977–1978	$306	$1,706	$378	$655	$2,700	$1,291	$512	$2,624	$984
1978–1979	$327	$1,831	$411	$688	$2,958	$1,397	$543	$2,867	$1,073
1979–1980	$355	$2,062	$451	$738	$3,225	$1,513	$583	$3,130	$1,163
1980–1981	$391	$2,413	$526	$804	$3,617	$1,679	$635	$3,498	$1,289
1981–1982	$434	$2,605	$590	$909	$4,113	$1,907	$714	$3,953	$1,457
1982–1983	$473	$3,008	$675	$1,031	$4,639	$2,139	$798	$4,439	$1,626
1983–1984	$528	$3,099	$730	$1,148	$5,093	$2,344	$891	$4,851	$1,783
1984–1985	$584	$3,485	$821	$1,228	$5,556	$2,567	$971	$5,315	$1,985
1985–1986	$641	$3,672	$888	$1,318	$6,121	$2,784	$1,045	$5,789	$2,181
1986–1987	$660	$3,684	$897	$1,414	$6,658	$3,042	$1,106	$6,316	$2,312
1987–1988	$706	$4,161	$809	$1,537	$7,116	$3,201	$1,218	$6,988	$2,458
1988–1989	$730	$4,817	$979	$1,646	$7,722	$3,472	$1,285	$7,461	$2,658
1989–1990	$756	$5,196	$978	$1,780	$8,396	$3,800	$1,356	$8,147	$2,839
1990–1991	$824	$5,570	$1,087	$1,888	$9,083	$4,009	$1,454	$8,772	$3,016
1991–1992	$936	$5,754	$1,189	$2,117	$9,759	$4,385	$1,628	$9,419	$3,286
1992–1993	$1,025	$6,059	$1,276	$2,349	$10,294	$4,752	$1,782	$9,942	$3,517
1993–1994	$1,125	$6,370	$1,399	$2,537	$10,952	$5,119	$1,942	$10,572	$3,827
1994–1995	$1,192	$6,914	$1,488	$2,681	$11,481	$5,391	$2,057	$11,111	$4,044
1995–1996	$1,239	$7,094	$1,522	$2,848	$12,243	$5,786	$2,179	$11,864	$4,338
1996–1997	$1,276	$7,236	$1,543	$2,987	$12,881	$6,118	$2,271	$12,498	$4,564
1997–1998	$1,314	$7,464	$1,695	$3,110	$13,344	$6,351	$2,360	$12,801	$4,755
1998–1999	$1,327	$7,854	$1,725	$3,229	$13,973	$6,723	$2,430	$13,428	$5,013
1999–2000	$1,338	$8,235	$1,721	$3,349	$14,588	$7,044	$2,506	$14,081	$5,238
2000–2001	$1,333	$9,067	$1,698	$3,501	$15,470	$7,372	$2,562	$15,000	$5,377
2001–2002	$1,379	$10,010	$1,772	$3,746	$16,287	$7,828	$2,727	$15,851	$5,719
% change 1976–1977 to 1981–1982	53.3%	63.6%	70.6%	47.5%	62.3%	56.5%	49.1%	60.2%	57.6%
% change 1981–1982 to 1991–1992	115.5%	120.9%	101.7%	132.8%	137.3%	129.9%	128.1%	138.3%	125.6%
% change 1991–1992 to 2001–2002	47.3%	74.0%	49.0%	77.0%	66.9%	78.5%	67.5%	68.3%	74.1%
% change 1976–1977 to 2001–2002	386.6%	528.8%	412.8%	507.6%	542.7%	542.4%	469.8%	542.6%	518.9%

Source: Snyder (2003)

Table 5.6

Average College Tuition and Fees: 1976–2002 (in constant 2001 dollars)

Academic Year	Community Colleges			4-Year Colleges			All Colleges		
	Public	Independent	Total	Public	Independent	Total	Public	Independent	Total
1976–1977	$882	$4,953	$1,075	$1,918	$7,883	$3,790	$1,489	$7,674	$2,875
1977–1978	$896	$4,984	$1,105	$1,913	$7,891	$3,774	$1,495	$7,667	$2,877
1978–1979	$888	$4,970	$1,115	$1,867	$8,029	$3,791	$1,473	$7,784	$2,912
1979–1980	$866	$5,030	$1,100	$1,799	$7,868	$3,691	$1,423	$7,637	$2,837
1980–1981	$841	$5,186	$1,130	$1,727	$7,773	$3,608	$1,364	$7,517	$2,769
1981–1982	$846	$5,072	$1,148	$1,771	$8,009	$3,714	$1,390	$7,696	$2,836
1982–1983	$868	$5,519	$1,238	$1,892	$8,511	$3,925	$1,464	$8,144	$2,983
1983–1984	$939	$5,508	$1,298	$2,040	$9,053	$4,166	$1,584	$8,622	$3,169
1984–1985	$996	$5,942	$1,400	$2,093	$9,472	$4,377	$1,655	$9,061	$3,385
1985–1986	$1,055	$6,045	$1,463	$2,169	$10,076	$4,584	$1,720	$9,529	$3,590
1986–1987	$1,067	$5,950	$1,449	$2,283	$10,754	$4,913	$1,787	$10,201	$3,734
1987–1988	$1,100	$6,483	$1,261	$2,395	$11,088	$4,987	$1,898	$10,889	$3,830
1988–1989	$1,093	$7,212	$1,466	$2,464	$11,560	$5,198	$1,923	$11,169	$3,978
1989–1990	$1,080	$7,423	$1,397	$2,542	$11,994	$5,429	$1,937	$11,638	$4,056
1990–1991	$1,117	$7,548	$1,474	$2,559	$12,308	$5,433	$1,970	$11,888	$4,087
1991–1992	$1,217	$7,480	$1,546	$2,752	$12,687	$5,701	$2,116	$12,245	$4,271
1992–1993	$1,294	$7,646	$1,610	$2,964	$12,990	$5,997	$2,248	$12,546	$4,438
1993–1994	$1,379	$7,808	$1,715	$3,109	$13,425	$6,275	$2,381	$12,959	$4,691
1994–1995	$1,425	$8,260	$1,777	$3,202	$13,715	$6,440	$2,457	$13,273	$4,832
1995–1996	$1,440	$8,243	$1,769	$3,309	$14,225	$6,723	$2,531	$13,785	$5,040
1996–1997	$1,440	$8,168	$1,742	$3,372	$14,540	$6,906	$2,564	$14,107	$5,152
1997–1998	$1,450	$8,234	$1,869	$3,430	$14,721	$7,006	$2,604	$14,121	$5,245
1998–1999	$1,441	$8,531	$1,874	$3,507	$15,178	$7,302	$2,640	$14,586	$5,445
1999–2000	$1,422	$8,753	$1,829	$3,560	$15,506	$7,487	$2,663	$14,967	$5,568
2000–2001	$1,370	$9,323	$1,746	$3,600	$15,908	$7,580	$2,635	$15,425	$5,529
2001–2002	$1,379	$10,010	$1,772	$3,746	$16,287	$7,828	$2,727	$15,851	$5,719
% change 1976–1977 to 1981–1982	-4.0%	2.4%	6.8%	-7.7%	1.6%	-2.0%	-6.7%	0.3%	-1.3%
% change 1981–1982 to 1991–1992	43.9%	47.5%	34.7%	55.4%	58.4%	53.5%	52.3%	59.1%	50.6%
% change 1991–1992 to 2001–2002	13.3%	33.8%	14.6%	36.1%	28.4%	37.3%	28.9%	29.4%	33.9%
% change 1976–1992 to 2001–2002	56.4%	102.1%	64.8%	95.3%	106.6%	106.5%	83.2%	106.6%	99.0%

Source: Snyder (2003)

Figure 5.3

College Tuition and Fees: 1976–2002

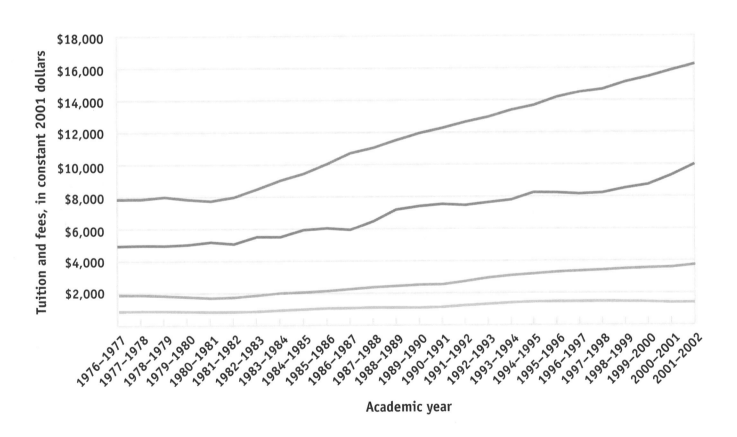

Source: Snyder (2003)

Table 5.7

Average In-State College Tuition and Fees: 2000–2001 and 2001–2002

State	Public Community Colleges			Public 4-Year Colleges			Independent 4-Year Colleges		
	2000–2001	2001–2002	% change	2000–2001	2001–2002	% change	2000–2001	2001–2002	% change
Alabama	$1,672	$1,990	19.0%	$2,987	$3,245	8.6%	$9,334	$10,229	9.6%
Alaska	$1,674	$1,717	2.6%	$2,941	$3,065	4.2%	$9,381	$9,852	5.0%
Arizona	$924	$962	4.2%	$2,346	$2,488	6.1%	$9,322	$9,759	4.7%
Arkansas	$1,158	$1,314	13.5%	$3,011	$3,387	12.5%	$9,109	$9,952	9.3%
California	$315	$315	0.1%	$2,566	$2,730	6.4%	$17,219	$18,399	6.9%
Colorado	$1,655	$1,685	1.9%	$2,980	$3,159	6.0%	$15,445	$16,245	5.2%
Connecticut	$1,868	$1,889	1.2%	$4,553	$4,772	4.8%	$20,056	$21,075	5.1%
Delaware	$1,680	$1,800	7.2%	$4,789	$5,065	5.8%	$8,415	$8,755	4.0%
District of Columbia	—	—	—	$2,070	$2,070	0.0%	$19,186	$20,093	4.7%
Florida	$1,438	$1,494	3.9%	$2,366	$2,555	8.0%	$13,805	$14,708	6.5%
Georgia	$1,260	$1,293	2.6%	$2,699	$2,838	5.2%	$13,770	$14,555	5.7%
Hawaii	$1,066	$1,067	0.1%	$2,968	$3,051	2.8%	$8,000	$8,777	9.7%
Idaho	$1,316	$1,410	7.2%	$2,628	$2,860	8.8%	$13,664	$5,326	-61.0%
Illinois	$1,532	$1,569	2.4%	$4,178	$4,567	9.3%	$15,317	$16,194	5.7%
Indiana	$2,108	$2,121	0.6%	$3,786	$4,002	5.7%	$16,078	$16,973	5.6%
Iowa	$2,141	$2,362	10.3%	$3,157	$3,470	9.9%	$14,630	$15,383	5.1%
Kansas	$1,378	$1,441	4.5%	$2,642	$2,700	2.2%	$11,206	$11,987	7.0%
Kentucky	$1,342	$1,561	16.3%	$2,898	$3,194	10.2%	$10,176	$10,972	7.8%
Louisiana	$935	$1,009	7.9%	$2,783	$2,865	2.9%	$15,591	$16,539	6.1%
Maine	$2,594	$2,642	1.8%	$4,267	$4,804	12.6%	$16,450	$17,619	7.1%
Maryland	$2,301	$2,244	-2.5%	$4,772	$4,973	4.2%	$18,621	$19,652	5.5%
Massachusetts	$1,894	$1,946	2.8%	$4,003	$3,999	-0.1%	$20,566	$21,526	4.7%
Michigan	$1,743	$1,780	2.2%	$4,615	$5,054	9.5%	$11,155	$11,802	5.8%
Minnesota	$2,507	$2,746	9.5%	$4,009	$4,494	12.1%	$16,243	$16,986	4.6%
Mississippi	$1,138	$1,362	19.6%	$2,969	$3,410	14.9%	$9,659	$10,004	3.6%
Missouri	$1,472	$1,498	1.8%	$3,879	$4,111	6.0%	$12,600	$13,218	4.9%
Montana	$2,004	$2,159	7.8%	$3,079	$3,467	12.6%	$9,631	$9,926	3.1%
Nebraska	$1,421	$1,498	5.4%	$3,101	$3,228	4.1%	$11,619	$14,074	21.1%
Nevada	$1,369	$1,410	3.0%	$2,344	$2,437	4.0%	$11,465	$13,510	17.8%
New Hampshire	$3,933	$4,324	10.0%	$6,458	$6,728	4.2%	$18,261	$19,186	5.1%
New Jersey	$2,295	$2,236	-2.6%	$5,609	$6,078	8.4%	$16,680	$17,403	4.3%

State	Public Community Colleges			Public 4-Year Colleges			Independent 4-Year Colleges		
	2000–2001	2001–2002	% change	2000–2001	2001–2002	% change	2000–2001	2001–2002	% change
New Mexico	$876	$921	5.0%	$2,627	$2,838	8.0%	$14,062	$14,499	3.1%
New York	$2,562	$2,584	0.9%	$4,063	$4,140	1.9%	$17,433	$18,357	5.3%
North Carolina	$896	$1,014	13.3%	$2,298	$2,646	15.1%	$14,274	$15,110	5.9%
North Dakota	$1,902	$2,090	9.9%	$2,942	$3,130	6.4%	$8,026	$8,362	4.2%
Ohio	$2,292	$2,373	3.6%	$4,742	$5,142	8.4%	$15,419	$16,259	5.4%
Oklahoma	$1,253	$1,214	-3.1%	$2,259	$2,373	5.0%	$10,587	$11,405	7.7%
Oregon	$1,637	$1,722	5.2%	$3,646	$3,862	5.9%	$17,533	$18,308	4.4%
Pennsylvania	$2,287	$2,369	3.6%	$5,917	$6,316	6.7%	$17,821	$18,796	5.5%
Rhode Island	$1,806	$1,854	2.7%	$4,506	$4,708	4.5%	$18,320	$19,177	4.7%
South Carolina	$1,467	$1,787	21.8%	$4,701	$5,502	17.0%	$12,713	$13,429	5.6%
South Dakota	$2,857	$2,964	3.7%	$3,484	$3,692	6.0%	$11,194	$11,796	5.4%
Tennessee	$1,441	$1,652	14.6%	$2,950	$3,340	13.2%	$12,922	$13,682	5.9%
Texas	$929	$981	5.6%	$2,785	$2,975	6.8%	$11,865	$12,728	7.3%
Utah	$1,571	$1,679	6.9%	$2,226	$2,388	7.3%	$3,754	$4,014	6.9%
Vermont	$3,004	$3,148	4.8%	$7,142	$7,470	4.6%	$15,740	$16,407	4.2%
Virginia	$1,132	$1,131	-0.1%	$3,723	$3,775	1.4%	$13,118	$13,892	5.9%
Washington	$1,758	$1,885	7.2%	$3,600	$3,788	5.2%	$15,874	$16,638	4.8%
West Virginia	$1,661	$1,661	0.0%	$2,551	$2,645	3.7%	$12,999	$13,136	1.1%
Wisconsin	$2,262	$2,310	2.1%	$3,417	$3,691	8.0%	$15,032	$15,907	5.8%
Wyoming	$1,440	$1,490	3.4%	$2,575	$2,807	9.0%	—	—	—
All states	$1,333	$1,379	3.5%	$3,501	$3,746	7.0%	$15,470	$16,287	5.3%

Source: Snyder (2003)

Table 5.8

Average In-State Tuition and Fees for Public Community Colleges: 1996–2002

| State | Academic Year | | | | | | % change 1996–2002 |
	1996–1997	1997–1998	1998–1999	1999–2000	2000–2001	2001–2002	
Alabama	$1,359	$1,343	$1,521	$1,486	$1,672	$1,990	46.4%
Alaska	$1,850	$1,900	$1,968	$2,028	$1,674	$1,717	-7.2%
Arizona	$783	$820	$857	$901	$924	$962	22.9%
Arkansas	$937	$942	$981	$1,059	$1,158	$1,314	40.3%
California	$371	$379	$396	$317	$315	$315	-15.1%
Colorado	$1,395	$1,449	$1,574	$1,548	$1,655	$1,685	20.8%
Connecticut	$1,722	$1,814	$1,814	$1,892	$1,868	$1,889	9.7%
Delaware	$1,330	$1,380	$1,440	$1,616	$1,680	$1,800	35.3%
Florida	$1,151	$1,252	$1,307	$1,330	$1,438	$1,494	29.8%
Georgia	$1,093	$1,153	$1,206	$1,384	$1,260	$1,293	18.3%
Hawaii	$789	$956	$1,004	$1,052	$1,066	$1,067	35.2%
Idaho	$1,043	$1,102	$1,186	$1,253	$1,316	$1,410	35.2%
Illinois	$1,290	$1,347	$1,424	$1,502	$1,532	$1,569	21.6%
Indiana	$2,331	$2,415	$2,124	$2,127	$2,108	$2,121	-9.0%
Iowa	$1,845	$1,885	$1,982	$2,060	$2,141	$2,362	28.0%
Kansas	$1,248	$1,285	$1,343	$1,310	$1,378	$1,441	15.4%
Kentucky	$1,215	$1,232	$1,240	$1,318	$1,342	$1,561	28.5%
Louisiana	$1,047	$1,080	$925	$876	$935	$1,009	-3.6%
Maine	$2,545	$2,594	$2,837	$2,586	$2,594	$2,642	3.8%
Maryland	$2,102	$2,171	$2,250	$2,262	$2,301	$2,244	6.8%
Massachusetts	$2,341	$2,221	$2,122	$1,926	$1,894	$1,946	-16.9%
Michigan	$1,576	$1,618	$1,680	$1,747	$1,743	$1,780	13.0%
Minnesota	$2,187	$2,245	$2,375	$2,359	$2,507	$2,746	25.6%
Mississippi	$954	$958	$968	$968	$1,138	$1,362	42.7%
Missouri	$1,281	$1,311	$1,411	$1,443	$1,472	$1,498	17.0%
Montana	$1,610	$1,713	$1,891	$1,961	$2,004	$2,159	34.1%

	Academic Year						
State	**1996–1997**	**1997–1998**	**1998–1999**	**1999–2000**	**2000–2001**	**2001–2002**	**% change 1996–2002**
Nebraska	$1,227	$1,267	$1,350	$1,372	$1,421	$1,498	22.1%
Nevada	$1,010	$1,106	$1,170	$1,208	$1,369	$1,410	39.6%
New Hampshire	$2,858	$3,177	$3,706	$3,744	$3,933	$4,324	51.3%
New Jersey	$1,949	$2,033	$2,054	$2,149	$2,295	$2,236	14.7%
New Mexico	$659	$679	$648	$823	$876	$921	39.7%
New York	$2,519	$2,576	$2,543	$2,554	$2,562	$2,584	2.6%
North Carolina	$581	$584	$585	$778	$896	$1,014	74.6%
North Dakota	$1,783	$1,798	$1,841	$1,893	$1,902	$2,090	17.2%
Ohio	$2,335	$2,388	$2,457	$2,377	$2,292	$2,373	1.6%
Oklahoma	$1,268	$1,285	$1,193	$1,239	$1,253	$1,214	-4.3%
Oregon	$1,526	$1,573	$1,629	$1,584	$1,637	$1,722	12.9%
Pennsylvania	$2,013	$2,098	$2,164	$2,115	$2,287	$2,369	17.7%
Rhode Island	$1,736	$1,746	$1,746	$1,746	$1,806	$1,854	6.8%
South Carolina	$1,114	$1,162	$1,220	$1,338	$1,467	$1,787	60.4%
South Dakota	$3,430	$3,930	$2,627	$2,747	$2,857	$2,964	-13.6%
Tennessee	$1,047	$1,133	$1,238	$1,314	$1,441	$1,652	57.8%
Texas	$791	$820	$890	$895	$929	$981	24.0%
Utah	$1,390	$1,439	$1,459	$1,500	$1,571	$1,679	20.8%
Vermont	$2,516	$2,616	$2,716	$2,846	$3,004	$3,148	25.1%
Virginia	$1,466	$1,475	$1,405	$1,140	$1,132	$1,131	-22.8%
Washington	$1,447	$1,516	$1,591	$1,649	$1,758	$1,885	30.3%
West Virginia	$1,373	$1,404	$1,473	$1,579	$1,661	$1,661	21.0%
Wisconsin	$1,947	$2,061	$2,115	$2,118	$2,262	$2,310	18.6%
Wyoming	$1,048	$1,157	$1,235	$1,320	$1,440	$1,490	42.1%
All states	$1,276	$1,318	$1,323	$1,336	$1,333	$1,379	8.1%

Source: Snyder (2003)

Table 5.9

Average In-State Tuition and Fees for Public Community Colleges, by State: 1996–2002 (in constant 2002 dollars)

State	Academic Year						% change 1996–2002
	1996–1997	1997–1998	1998–1999	1999–2000	2000–2001	2001–2002	
Alabama	$1,527	$1,479	$1,649	$1,572	$1,710	$1,990	30.3%
Alaska	$2,079	$2,092	$2,134	$2,146	$1,712	$1,717	-17.4%
Arizona	$880	$903	$929	$953	$944	$962	9.3%
Arkansas	$1,053	$1,037	$1,063	$1,121	$1,184	$1,314	24.8%
California	$417	$417	$429	$335	$322	$315	-24.5%
Colorado	$1,568	$1,596	$1,706	$1,638	$1,692	$1,685	7.5%
Connecticut	$1,935	$1,998	$1,967	$2,002	$1,910	$1,889	-2.4%
Delaware	$1,495	$1,520	$1,561	$1,710	$1,718	$1,800	20.4%
Florida	$1,294	$1,379	$1,417	$1,407	$1,471	$1,494	15.5%
Georgia	$1,228	$1,270	$1,308	$1,464	$1,289	$1,293	5.3%
Hawaii	$887	$1,053	$1,088	$1,113	$1,091	$1,067	20.3%
Idaho	$1,172	$1,214	$1,286	$1,325	$1,346	$1,410	20.3%
Illinois	$1,450	$1,483	$1,543	$1,590	$1,567	$1,569	8.2%
Indiana	$2,620	$2,660	$2,303	$2,251	$2,156	$2,121	-19.0%
Iowa	$2,074	$2,076	$2,149	$2,180	$2,189	$2,362	13.9%
Kansas	$1,403	$1,415	$1,456	$1,387	$1,409	$1,441	2.7%
Kentucky	$1,365	$1,357	$1,344	$1,395	$1,372	$1,561	14.3%
Louisiana	$1,177	$1,189	$1,003	$927	$956	$1,009	-14.2%
Maine	$2,860	$2,857	$3,076	$2,736	$2,653	$2,642	-7.6%
Maryland	$2,362	$2,391	$2,440	$2,394	$2,353	$2,244	-5.0%
Massachusetts	$2,631	$2,446	$2,301	$2,038	$1,937	$1,946	-26.0%
Michigan	$1,771	$1,782	$1,822	$1,849	$1,782	$1,780	0.5%
Minnesota	$2,458	$2,472	$2,575	$2,496	$2,564	$2,746	11.7%
Mississippi	$1,072	$1,055	$1,050	$1,024	$1,164	$1,362	27.0%
Missouri	$1,440	$1,444	$1,530	$1,527	$1,505	$1,498	4.1%
Montana	$1,809	$1,886	$2,050	$2,075	$2,049	$2,159	19.3%

| | Academic Year | | | | | | % change |
State	1996–1997	1997–1998	1998–1999	1999–2000	2000–2001	2001–2002	1996–2002
Nebraska	$1,379	$1,395	$1,464	$1,451	$1,453	$1,498	8.6%
Nevada	$1,135	$1,218	$1,269	$1,279	$1,400	$1,410	24.2%
New Hampshire	$3,212	$3,499	$4,018	$3,961	$4,022	$4,324	34.6%
New Jersey	$2,190	$2,239	$2,227	$2,274	$2,347	$2,236	2.1%
New Mexico	$741	$748	$702	$871	$896	$921	24.3%
New York	$2,831	$2,837	$2,757	$2,702	$2,620	$2,584	-8.7%
North Carolina	$653	$643	$634	$823	$916	$1,014	55.3%
North Dakota	$2,004	$1,980	$1,997	$2,003	$1,945	$2,090	4.3%
Ohio	$2,624	$2,630	$2,664	$2,515	$2,344	$2,373	-9.6%
Oklahoma	$1,425	$1,415	$1,294	$1,311	$1,281	$1,214	-14.8%
Oregon	$1,715	$1,732	$1,766	$1,676	$1,674	$1,722	0.4%
Pennsylvania	$2,262	$2,310	$2,347	$2,237	$2,339	$2,369	4.7%
Rhode Island	$1,951	$1,923	$1,893	$1,847	$1,847	$1,854	-5.0%
South Carolina	$1,252	$1,280	$1,323	$1,416	$1,500	$1,787	42.7%
South Dakota	$3,855	$4,328	$2,849	$2,907	$2,922	$2,964	-23.1%
Tennessee	$1,177	$1,248	$1,343	$1,391	$1,474	$1,652	40.4%
Texas	$889	$903	$965	$947	$950	$981	10.3%
Utah	$1,562	$1,585	$1,582	$1,587	$1,607	$1,679	7.5%
Vermont	$2,828	$2,881	$2,945	$3,011	$3,072	$3,148	11.3%
Virginia	$1,648	$1,624	$1,523	$1,206	$1,158	$1,131	-31.3%
Washington	$1,626	$1,670	$1,725	$1,745	$1,798	$1,885	15.9%
West Virginia	$1,543	$1,546	$1,597	$1,670	$1,699	$1,661	7.7%
Wisconsin	$2,188	$2,270	$2,293	$2,241	$2,313	$2,310	5.6%
Wyoming	$1,178	$1,274	$1,339	$1,397	$1,473	$1,490	26.5%
All states	$1,434	$1,451	$1,434	$1,420	$1,370	$1,379	-3.8%

Source: Snyder (1999, 2003); Snyder & Hoffman (2001)

Table 5.10

Percentage of Federal Student Aid Received by Public Community Colleges: 1991–2003

Academic Year	Federal Student Aid			
	Pell grant	Campus-based aid	Stafford subsidized loans	Stafford unsubsidized loans
1991–1992	24.3%	9.3%	6.4%	—
1992–1993	25.7%	9.7%	6.3%	6.7%
1993–1994	30.0%	9.6%	6.1%	4.3%
1994–1995	32.7%	9.7%	5.9%	4.9%
1995–1996	32.7%	9.6%	5.8%	5.1%
1996–1997	33.0%	9.8%	5.8%	5.0%
1997–1998	32.8%	9.9%	5.8%	5.0%
1998–1999	32.4%	9.9%	5.7%	4.7%
1999–2000	33.4%	9.8%	5.5%	4.4%
2000–2001	33.7%	9.8%	5.4%	4.4%
2001–2002	35.0%	9.8%	—	—
2002–2003	34.7%	9.0%	6.3%	5.3%
10-year change	9.0%	-0.7%	0.0%	5.3%

Source: College Board (2004, Table 5)

Figure 5.4

**Public Community College Share of Pell Grant Dollars:
1991–2003**

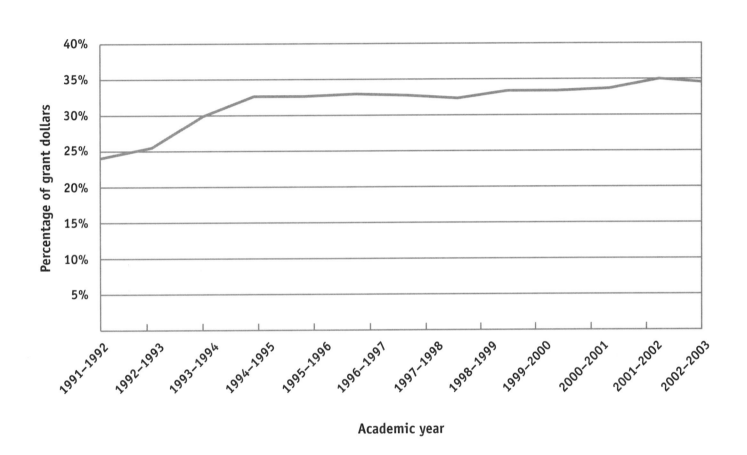

Academic year

Source: College Board (2004)

Figure 5.5
Authorized and Actual Maximum Pell Grant Awards: 1973–2004

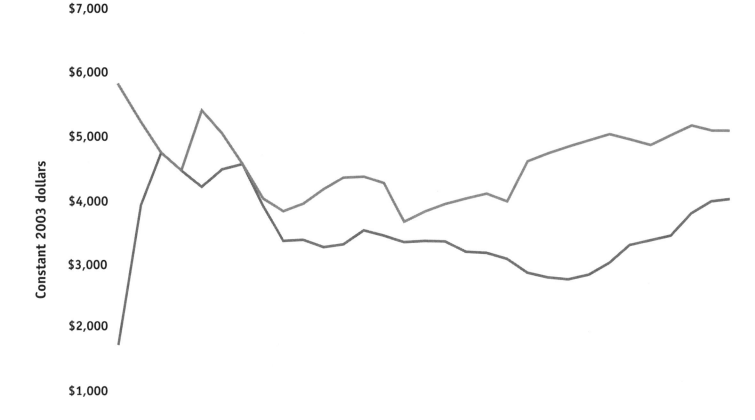

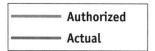

Source: College Board (2004)

Table 5.11
Authorized and Actual Maximum Pell Grant Awards: 1973–2004

Academic Year	Current Dollars		Constant 2003 Dollars	
	Authorized	Actual	Authorized	Actual
1973–1974	$1,400	$452	$5,739	$1,853
1974–1975	$1,400	$1,050	$5,207	$3,905
1975–1976	$1,400	$1,400	$4,727	$4,727
1976–1977	$1,400	$1,400	$4,450	$4,450
1977–1978	$1,800	$1,400	$5,391	$4,193
1978–1979	$1,800	$1,600	$5,029	$4,470
1979–1980	$1,800	$1,800	$4,553	$4,553
1980–1981	$1,800	$1,750	$4,011	$3,899
1981–1982	$1,900	$1,670	$3,813	$3,352
1982–1983	$2,100	$1,800	$3,932	$3,370
1983–1984	$2,300	$1,800	$4,162	$3,257
1984–1985	$2,500	$1,900	$4,345	$3,302
1985–1986	$2,600	$2,100	$4,360	$3,521
1986–1987	$2,600	$2,100	$4,259	$3,440
1987–1988	$2,300	$2,100	$3,658	$3,340
1988–1989	$2,500	$2,200	$3,818	$3,360
1989–1990	$2,700	$2,300	$3,937	$3,354
1990–1991	$2,900	$2,300	$4,024	$3,191
1991–1992	$3,100	$2,400	$4,101	$3,175
1992–1993	$3,100	$2,400	$3,981	$3,082
1993–1994	$3,700	$2,300	$4,612	$2,867
1994–1995	$3,900	$2,300	$4,737	$2,794
1995–1996	$4,100	$2,340	$4,844	$2,765
1996–1967	$4,300	$2,470	$4,942	$2,839
1997–1998	$4,500	$2,700	$5,039	$3,024
1998–1999	$4,500	$3,000	$4,959	$3,306
1999–2000	$4,500	$3,125	$4,872	$3,383
2000–2001	$4,800	$3,300	$5,028	$3,457
2001–2002	$5,100	$3,750	$5,179	$3,808
2002–2003	$5,100	$4,000	$5,100	$4,000
2003–2004	$5,100	$4,050	$5,100	$4,050

Source: College Board (2004, Table 8)

Table 5.12

Percentage of Full-Time Undergraduates Who Received Grants, by Source of Grant: 1989–1990 and 1999–2000

College Type	1989–1990		1999–2000	
	% receiving	Average amount	% receiving	Average amount
Pell grant				
Public community college	20%	$1,700	24%	$2,200[a]
Public 4-year college	21%	$2,100	22%	$2,200
Private, nonprofit 4-year college	24%	$2,100	23%	$2,100
Private, for-profit less-than-4-year college	49%	$2,200	51%	$2,200
State grant				
Public community college	11%	$1,000	18%[a]	$1,200
Public 4-year college	14%	$1,400	21%[a]	$2,000[a]
Private, nonprofit 4-year college	25%	$2,500	26%	$2,700
Private, for-profit less-than-4-year college	9%	$2,800	18%[a]	$1,900[a]
Institutional grant				
Public community college	10%	$900	16%[a]	$900
Public 4-year college	15%	$2,400	24%[a]	$2,900[a]
Private, nonprofit 4-year college	49%	$4,900	65%[a]	$7,600[a]
Private, for-profit less-than-4-year college	6%	$2,100	10%	$1,000[a]

Source: Choy (2004)

Note. Numbers are expressed in constant 1999 dollars.

[a]Statistically significant change between academic years, 1989–2000.

Table 5.13
Percentage of Undergraduates Who Received Financial Aid, by Dependency Status: 2003–2004

College Type and Dependency Status	All aid	Grants	Loans (excluding PLUS)	Work-study	Federal aid	Federal grants	Federal loans	State aid
Public community college								
Dependent	42.7%	35.4%	12.3%	3.7%	28.0%	19.7%	11.3%	13.0%
Independent, no dependent, unmarried	45.0%	36.8%	13.6%	3.4%	26.9%	19.5%	13.2%	10.4%
Independent, no dependent, married	40.3%	30.9%	7.3%	2.1%	12.5%	6.6%	6.6%	7.2%
Independent with dependents	54.0%	48.6%	12.4%	3.7%	36.2%	33.1%	11.8%	13.8%
Total	46.8%	39.8%	12.1%	3.5%	29.2%	23.1%	11.3%	12.3%
Public 4-year college								
Dependent	69.2%	50.7%	44.7%	10.0%	51.9%	21.8%	42.9%	22.2%
Independent, no dependent, unmarried	69.2%	52.5%	49.0%	6.4%	55.4%	35.3%	47.5%	15.3%
Independent, no dependent, married	58.2%	38.6%	36.7%	4.6%	41.8%	18.3%	35.0%	9.3%
Independent with dependents	70.1%	60.9%	42.7%	5.2%	52.9%	43.5%	41.4%	16.5%
Total	68.6%	51.7%	44.5%	8.5%	51.9%	26.6%	42.8%	19.6%
Independent nonprofit 4-year college								
Dependent	85.1%	77.7%	60.3%	30.3%	66.5%	24.8%	58.1%	25.0%
Independent, no dependent, unmarried	78.5%	63.7%	54.0%	9.6%	59.2%	31.8%	51.7%	16.8%
Independent, no dependent, married	77.1%	61.3%	42.9%	5.9%	49.1%	18.5%	42.1%	10.3%
Independent with dependents	82.6%	69.6%	49.3%	3.8%	57.4%	39.7%	48.1%	22.4%
Total	83.3%	73.5%	56.3%	21.1%	62.8%	28.2%	54.4%	22.6%
Proprietary college								
Dependent	85.2%	59.7%	72.6%	4.1%	80.0%	48.4%	69.9%	12.4%
Independent, no dependent, unmarried	89.7%	56.3%	77.6%	1.8%	82.2%	39.9%	75.8%	9.9%
Independent, no dependent, married	84.3%	45.7%	65.4%	1.3%	69.0%	21.9%	64.6%	8.0%
Independent with dependents	92.0%	76.9%	73.4%	1.7%	83.9%	66.7%	72.2%	8.7%
Total	89.2%	65.7%	73.4%	2.3%	81.4%	52.8%	71.8%	9.8%
Multiple colleges[a]								
Dependent	64.9%	44.3%	43.6%	9.4%	51.0%	22.7%	41.8%	12.3%
Independent, no dependent, unmarried	67.3%	47.3%	45.5%	6.6%	52.4%	28.4%	44.0%	9.8%
Independent, no dependent, married	57.0%	36.3%	30.4%	1.8%	35.2%	12.5%	29.5%	7.9%
Independent with dependents	71.2%	57.8%	42.7%	3.7%	53.1%	40.2%	41.1%	9.5%
Total	66.3%	47.6%	42.7%	7.0%	50.6%	27.3%	41.1%	10.9%
All colleges								
Dependent	63.8%	50.3%	38.1%	11.2%	47.8%	22.8%	36.4%	18.6%
Independent, no dependent, unmarried	61.8%	46.9%	37.0%	4.9%	46.1%	28.0%	35.8%	12.4%
Independent, no dependent, married	53.3%	37.5%	24.7%	3.0%	29.7%	12.4%	23.7%	8.2%
Independent with dependents	65.9%	57.2%	31.3%	3.7%	48.7%	40.6%	30.4%	14.2%
Total	63.2%	50.7%	35.0%	7.5%	46.4%	27.6%	33.7%	15.6%

Source: NCES (2005)

[a]Students who attended more than one college in the 2003–2004 academic year.

Table 5.14

Amount of Financial Aid Received by Undergraduates, by Dependency Status: 2003–2004

College Type and Dependency Status	Total Aid Received							
	Total aid	Grants	Loans (excluding PLUS)	Work-study	Federal aid	Federal grants	Federal loans	State aid
Public community college								
Dependent	$3,154	$2,415	$2,853	$1,915	$2,923	$2,334	$2,460	$1,206
Independent, no dependent, unmarried	$3,424	$1,866	$4,436	$2,194	$3,764	$2,022	$4,212	$1,076
Independent, no dependent, married	$2,244	$1,399	$4,072	$1,700	$3,163	$1,815	$3,808	$1,086
Independent with dependents	$3,291	$2,194	$4,022	$2,183	$3,544	$2,261	$3,936	$1,041
Total	$3,177	$2,161	$3,638	$2,047	$3,331	$2,240	$3,412	$1,116
Public 4-year college								
Dependent	$7,645	$4,365	$4,973	$2,038	$6,097	$2,698	$4,263	$2,512
Independent, no dependent, unmarried	$8,201	$3,432	$6,988	$2,217	$7,674	$2,569	$6,750	$2,022
Independent, no dependent, married	$6,501	$2,794	$6,797	$2,006	$6,776	$2,262	$6,736	$2,184
Independent with dependents	$7,359	$3,340	$6,584	$1,876	$7,614	$2,754	$6,489	$1,865
Total	$7,618	$3,988	$5,593	$2,042	$6,584	$2,669	$5,078	$2,372
Independent nonprofit 4-year college								
Dependent	$15,616	$9,236	$6,734	$1,807	$7,983	$2,650	$4,647	$3,092
Independent, no dependent, unmarried	$10,382	$5,406	$8,088	$1,989	$8,023	$2,599	$7,165	$2,422
Independent, no dependent, married	$8,037	$4,288	$7,449	$1,890	$6,994	$2,626	$6,807	$2,458
Independent with dependents	$8,182	$4,367	$6,873	$1,958	$7,385	$2,595	$6,460	$2,288
Total	$13,142	$7,676	$6,943	$1,823	$7,831	$2,626	$5,349	$2,858
Proprietary college								
Dependent	$10,037	$3,780	$6,010	$2,361	$7,962	$2,594	$4,610	$3,011
Independent, no dependent, unmarried	$8,876	$2,922	$7,756	$2,589	$7,233	$2,362	$6,554	$2,510
Independent, no dependent, married	$8,496	$3,220	$7,872	ns	$7,276	$2,290	$6,956	$3,670
Independent with dependents	$8,156	$3,197	$6,473	$2,642	$7,339	$2,627	$6,001	$2,840
Total	$8,767	$3,275	$6,759	$2,515	$7,458	$2,567	$5,875	$2,878
Multiple colleges[a]								
Dependent	$7,395	$4,114	$4,787	$1,738	$6,051	$2,600	$4,060	$2,128
Independent, no dependent, unmarried	$7,507	$2,890	$7,243	$2,118	$7,284	$2,458	$6,915	$1,597
Independent, no dependent, married	$5,867	$2,281	$7,444	ns	$6,699	$2,221	$6,972	$1,146
Independent with dependents	$6,826	$2,937	$6,493	$2,549	$7,006	$2,582	$6,253	$1,499
Total	$7,166	$3,462	$5,764	$1,912	$6,538	$2,559	$5,245	$1,864
All colleges								
Dependent	$8,594	$5,163	$5,282	$1,901	$6,065	$2,573	$4,195	$2,350
Independent, no dependent, unmarried	$7,023	$3,073	$6,949	$2,170	$6,600	$2,366	$6,375	$1,768
Independent, no dependent, married	$5,345	$2,485	$6,801	$1,918	$6,136	$2,203	$6,404	$1,820
Independent with dependents	$5,786	$2,899	$6,032	$2,143	$5,840	$2,484	$5,765	$1,589
Total	$7,350	$4,018	$5,816	$1,961	$6,085	$2,492	$5,055	$2,071

Source: NCES (2005)

[a]Students who attended more than one college in the 2003–2004 academic year.

Table 5.15
Average Tuition for Full-Time Community College Students, by Dependency Status and Family Income: Selected Academic Years, 1989–2004

Dependency Status and Family Income	Average Tuition[a]					Average Net Tuition[b]				
	1989–1990	1992–1993	1995–1996	1999–2000	2003–2004	1989–1990	1992–1993	1995–1996	1999–2000	2003–2004
Dependency status										
Dependent students	$1,200	$1,500	$1,600	$1,700	$2,000	$900	$1,100	$1,100	$1,100	$1,300
Independent students	$1,300	$1,500	$1,700	$1,600	$1,900	$500	$600	$800	$700	$800
Unmarried, no dependents	$1,300	$1,500	$2,000	$1,700	$1,900	$700	$700	$1,400	$900	$1,000
Married, not dependents	$1,000	$1,600	$2,100	$1,600	$2,200	$700	$1,100	$1,500	$1,100	$1,500
Unmarried with dependents	$1,200	$1,500	$1,500	$1,400	$1,800	$100	$300	$400	$400	$500
Married, with dependents	$1,300	$1,600	$1,500	$1,600	$2,000	$600	$600	$400	$600	$800
Family income										
Dependent students										
Lowest quarter	$1,000	$1,500	$1,500	$1,700	$1,800	$300	$500	$500	$600	$500
Lower middle quarter	$1,300	$1,500	$1,600	$1,900	$2,000	$1,000	$1,100	$1,100	$1,300	$1,300
Upper middle quarter	$1,300	$1,500	$1,700	$1,800	$2,100	$1,100	$1,400	$1,500	$1,500	$1,700
Highest quarter	$1,200	$1,500	$1,600	$1,600	$2,100	$1,100	$1,400	$1,400	$1,400	$1,800
Independent students										
Lowest quarter	$1,300	$1,500	$1,700	$1,500	$1,800	$400	$300	$500	$400	$500
Lower middle quarter	$1,300	$1,700	$1,800	$1,600	$1,900	$600	$900	$1,000	$700	$700
Upper middle quarter	$1,100	$1,300	$1,500	$1,700	$2,000	$500	$800	$800	$1,000	$1,100
Highest quarter	$1,200	$1,600	$1,900	$1,400	$2,100	$900	$1,200	$1,500	$1,200	$1,800
Total, all students	$1,200	$1,500	$1,600	$1,700	$2,000	$700	$900	$1,000	$1,000	$1,100

Source: NCES (2004j, 2005)

Note. Numbers are expressed in constant 2003 dollars.

[a]Includes all tuition and fees charged by the college. Averages include fees charged to out-of-district and out-of-state students.

[b]Tuition and fees minus grant aid received. Where grant aid was greater than tuition and fees, the value was set to zero.

Table 5.16

Average Price of Attendance and Expected Family Contribution
for Full-Time Community College Students, by Dependency Status
and Family Income: Selected Academic Years, 1989–2004

Dependency Status and Family Income	Average Price of Attendance[a]					Average Net Price of Attendance[b]				
	1989–1990	1992–1993	1995–1996	1999–2000	2003–2004	1989–1990	1992–1993	1995–1996	1999–2000	2003–2004
Dependency status										
Dependent students	$8,100	$8,400	$8,200	$9,400	$9,800	$7,200	$7,500	$7,000	$7,700	$7,800
Independent students	$10,600	$9,500	$9,900	$11,000	$11,200	$7,900	$7,000	$7,300	$7,800	$7,300
Unmarried, no dependents	$10,300	$9,600	$10,200	$10,900	$11,000	$8,100	$7,600	$7,800	$8,100	$7,500
Married, no dependents	$10,000	$9,600	$10,000	$11,200	$12,000	$8,600	$8,100	$8,400	$9,700	$9,900
Unmarried, with dependents	$10,900	$9,300	$9,700	$10,700	$10,900	$6,200	$5,700	$6,700	$7,000	$6,200
Married, with dependents	$11,000	$9,600	$9,900	$11,200	$11,600	$8,500	$6,700	$6,800	$7,300	$7,400
Family income										
Dependent students										
Lowest quarter	$8,000	$8,300	$7,700	$9,200	$9,500	$5,900	$6,300	$5,300	$6,200	$6,000
Lower middle quarter	$8,400	$8,100	$8,300	$9,500	$9,800	$7,600	$7,200	$7,300	$8,000	$7,900
Upper middle quarter	$8,200	$9,000	$8,400	$9,500	$10,100	$7,800	$8,600	$7,800	$8,700	$8,800
Highest quarter	$7,600	$8,300	$8,200	$9,600	$10,000	$7,400	$8,100	$7,900	$8,900	$8,900
Independent students										
Lowest quarter	$10,500	$9,500	$9,800	$10,800	$11,000	$7,100	$6,200	$6,500	$6,600	$6,200
Lower middle quarter	$10,700	$9,700	$10,400	$10,800	$11,200	$8,300	$7,700	$7,200	$7,400	$6,700
Upper middle quarter	$10,700	$9,200	$9,900	$11,500	$11,400	$8,200	$7,100	$7,800	$9,300	$8,000
Highest quarter	$10,300	$9,600	$9,500	$11,200	$11,700	$9,000	$8,600	$8,700	$10,000	$10,200
Total, all students	$9,100	$8,800	$8,800	$10,000	$10,400	$7,500	$7,300	$7,100	$7,800	$7,600

	Average Expected Family Contribution[c]				
Dependency Status and Family Income	**1989–1990**	**1992–1993**	**1995–1996**	**1999–2000**	**2003–2004**
Dependency status					
Dependent students	$10,200	$9,800	$8,100	$9,600	$10,200
Independent students	$3,800	$3,600	$4,700	$4,300	$3,200
Unmarried, no dependents	$7,300	$5,900	$5,000	$4,500	$3,300
Married, no dependents	$2,500	$4,000	$10,300	$12,000	$11,900
Unmarried, with dependents	$700	$500	$1,500	$1,100	$700
Married, with dependents	$2,200	$2,700	$4,600	$3,900	$3,200
Family income					
Dependent students					
Lowest quarter	$3,200	$2,800	$1,200	$1,200	$1,000
Lower middle quarter	$7,200	$6,400	$4,400	$6,100	$5,400
Upper middle quarter	$13,200	$8,600	$10,500	$12,200	$12,000
Highest quarter	$21,100	$27,000	$19,900	$26,600	$29,700
Independent students					
Lowest quarter	$1,900	$1,600	$500	$500	$300
Lower middle quarter	$4,200	$3,600	$2,200	$2,200	$1,300
Upper middle quarter	$3,600	$3,700	$5,600	$6,600	$4,400
Highest quarter	$9,100	$9,600	$18,400	$17,500	$14,100
Total, all students	$7,700	$7,300	$7,000	$7,600	$7,600

Source: NCES (2005); Wei, Li, & Berkner (2004)

Note. Numbers are expressed in constant 2003 dollars.

[a]Average price of attendance includes tuition, fees, books, supplies, room and board, transportation, and personal expenses, based on institutionally estimated budgets.

[b]Average net price of attendance equals price of attendance minus grant and loan aid received. Includes students who received no financial aid.

[c]Federal expected family contribution is the amount students and families are expected to contribute to the price of attendance at a postsecondary institution, based on federal needs analysis.

Figure 5.6
Average Financial Need of Full-Time, Full-Year Dependent Undergraduates: 1989–1990 and 1999–2000

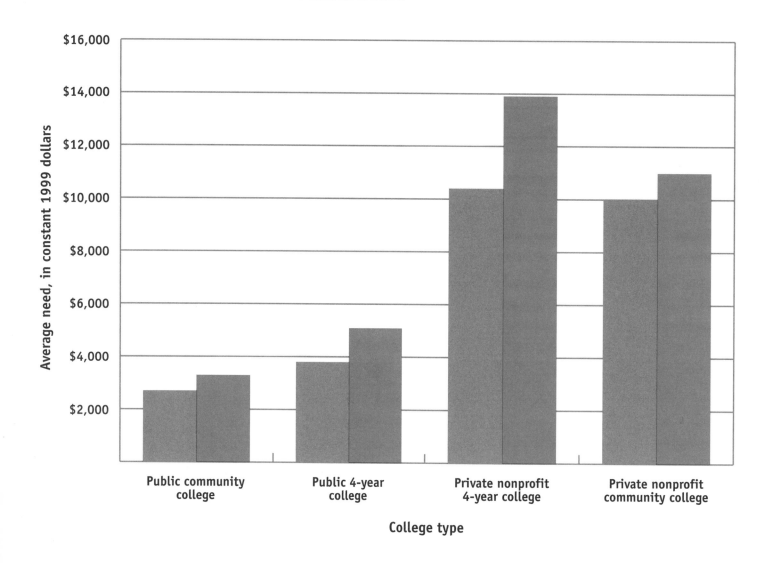

Legend:
- 1989–1990
- 1999–2000

Y-axis: Average need, in constant 1999 dollars

X-axis (College type): Public community college, Public 4-year college, Private nonprofit 4-year college, Private nonprofit community college

Source: Choy (2004)

Note. Amounts reported for 1999–2000 represent statistically significant change from 1989–1990.

VI

A Look at the Future

Over the past 100 years, community colleges have weathered many challenges in their evolution from small colleges with limited reach and missions centered on transfer and vocational training to the large, sophisticated educational enterprises of today. Now, at the beginning of a second century of service, they are evolving into mature organizations with comprehensive missions and a clearly recognized position in the American education system. And they are being recognized by national and community leaders as innovative colleges that are critical to the economic and cultural well-being of their communities and the nation as a whole. These colleges are located squarely at the center of the continuum that begins with early childhood education and K–12 schools and extends through college, graduate programs, and lifelong learning.

Moreover, in an era of globalization when American competitiveness in world markets depends on a workforce educated to perform effectively in a knowledge economy, community colleges play a critical role. They develop the nation's human capital, thus contributing directly to national productivity, raising incomes and tax revenues, and building economic capacity. With most modern jobs requiring at least some college education as well as current skills, these engines of economic growth help to close the participation gap by ensuring that people of all social levels—from new immigrants to laid off workers to people who already hold advanced degrees—have access to job training so they can become productive members of American society. To a great extent, then, as these people's colleges go, so goes the nation.

The mature state of today's community colleges presents a moment of choice. In the life of any organization, reaching maturity requires choosing a course of action: Either continue to do what was successful in the past and hope to avoid stagnation, or respond to new environmental conditions with creativity and innovation and perhaps become something different in the process. The choice community colleges will make depends on a number of issues that can be sorted into several broad categories: new student demographics, teaching and learning, workforce development, credentialing, funding, and public policy.

The changing face of the nation is also the changing face of community colleges, as people of all backgrounds and ages use these colleges to meet their education goals. By 2015, the traditional college-age population is expected to grow from 26 million to 30 million, with Hispanics accounting for 49% of the increase. The states of California, Texas, New York, Florida, and Georgia will experience the highest growth in this age group. Because of their position as a preferred entry point into higher education for Hispanics and other students of color, community colleges can expect to see higher absolute numbers as well as more diversity in their student bodies. At the same time, greater numbers of adults—including recent immigrants, international students, and senior citizens—will also seek their services. In the next decade, community colleges can expect an overall enrollment increase of about 13%. However, budget challenges that have plagued community colleges for decades have already resulted in the open door closing for some students in California and Florida. Community colleges must strive to find alternatives to ensure that access to higher education is available to those who want it.

In conjunction with changing student demographics at community colleges, the need for basic skills instruction and remediation will continue to be a controversial issue. The commitment to the open door presumes a commitment to provide the support students need to succeed, and this often means bringing their reading, writing, and mathematical skills up to a point where they can manage college studies. Community colleges have readily assumed the task of providing this type of instruction because they understand that persistence and success depend on the requisite skills foundation. This stance has placed considerable stress on available resources that continue to decrease as other social needs grow. Therefore, the coming years provide an optimal time for community colleges to make stronger connections

with K–12 to better align curriculum to ensure that exiting students are better prepared for college-level work. Acknowledging that postsecondary education or training is essential and providing appropriate funding to ensure universal access, be it into remedial academic work, workforce training, or general education is an urgent matter that community college leaders and policymakers must address.

The core mission of community colleges will continue to be teaching and learning, and the needs of a new mix of students combined with the emergence of new technologies will certainly affect how those fundamental processes are carried out. In fact, many of the instructional developments discussed in this chapter are already under way. Within the context of the learning college concept—whether or not colleges formally adopt this approach—greater emphasis will be placed on multiple instructional delivery modes. Faculty will evolve from traditional lecturers into learning facilitators who use new technologies to personalize instruction for each student. Active and collaborative learning will be the norm, and outcomes assessment will be a part of each learning experience. The learning environment will be all-encompassing, including not just the classroom and college campus, but

the work and living spaces of students and even cyberspace. Today, the general population's access to massive amounts of information via the Internet has transformed the learning enterprise, and full implementation of wireless technology in the near future will enhance instructional capacity even more. Support services will also continue to evolve, particularly as the Web and new technologies expand the ways these services can be delivered.

Distributed or distance education can be expected to grow exponentially as more students combine this format with face-to-face courses. Distance education has already erased some of the traditional boundaries observed by higher education in the past. In the future the global reach of local colleges will be a reality as people around the world select courses on the basis of their immediate education needs rather than proximity to a college. The low cost of community colleges will make this option even more attractive. Web-based instruction will also be used increasingly in continuing education for students who want noncredit, subject-specific instruction to upgrade job skills and for employers needing training for their employees. The continued expansion of distance education will require that colleges have state-of-the-art equipment, sufficient technical support, and appropriate security measures in place. Also, every faculty member will have to be highly skilled in developing and delivering instruction by this means. Finally, local and state policies regarding funding and tuition structures will need to be reassessed because geographic borders are no longer meaningful delineators.

In a world where workforce development has become the primary mandate for all higher education institutions, community colleges will continue to stand in the vanguard. Their ability to rapidly design and implement curriculums for emerging career fields has always given them a competitive edge over other education providers. For that reason, courses in fields such as bioterrorism, complementary health services, and nanotechnology can all be found at community colleges today. The colleges can be expected to continue this rapid curricular response in the future as societal and technological developments lead to the creation of career fields unimagined today.

The accelerating pace of modern life has caused great pressure to reduce the time needed for workforce preparation. In order to minimize time in training, community colleges must resolve the disconnections that exist in American education today. Their current efforts to establish career pathways beginning in high school and continuing with seamless transfer to the baccalaureate and graduate levels are a good start, but much remains to be done. Likewise, there are many examples of two- and four-year colleges working together to provide a seamless transition from one to the other. These include locating four-year campuses at two-year colleges so that working adults can finish a bachelor's degree without moving, designing common course numbering systems between colleges, and implementing articulation agreements that guarantee the transfer of credits.

Although many traditional boundaries have disappeared with the advent of the Internet and the practices just described, there is still a sense that the various education sectors are operating independently of each other. For that reason, students may graduate from high school without the requisite skills for college work, and many community college students still have difficulty transferring all the credits they have earned to a four-year college or university. High school students in dual-enrollment programs may find that the courses are not transferable because baccalaureate-granting colleges question the academic rigor of such studies. People who engage in noncredit continuing education courses and professional development workshops, or who study at a for-profit college, may not be able to count these studies toward a desired degree.

Because many of these students arrive first at the doors of community colleges, these colleges will need to take leadership in bringing together all parties to resolve the problem of transferring for-credit and noncredit learning experiences and applying these to degree requirements. Together, K–12 educators and representatives from two- and four-year colleges, for-profit education providers, corporations, and others will need to design an education network in which all types of learning activities can be validated and students can move readily among sectors to achieve their educational goals. Discussions about academic credentialing are already occurring, and there are many proponents of a national transcript bank where students can deposit information on any learning activity they undertake over a lifetime. Students could then give permission to educators, employers, and others who need access to the complete learning record.

Changing public policy will be the key to resolving many of the issues that may affect community colleges in the future. First and foremost, policymakers must address the need for adequate funding if they expect the American education system to produce workers who are fully prepared to compete in a global economy. And, rather than pitting different sectors of the education system against each other in a battle for scarce resources, policymakers must see—and fund—education as a continuum of services that citizens will access throughout their lives. For many states this will entail resolving the structural deficits that hamper their ability to provide the social capital their citizens need.

Whatever the future levels of public funding, there will be greater expectations for accountability. Community colleges will have to expand their capacity to collect and use data in order to respond to public inquiries about institutional effectiveness and learning. Particularly in times when state revenues are in a down cycle and the demand for social services is growing, colleges will need to demonstrate the value added for tax dollars spent. It will also be critically important that community college leaders participate in policy discussions about appropriate indicators and incentives for effective performance. Finally,

these leaders will need to ensure that accountability mandates ultimately benefit students. Data gathered for accountability purposes must be used to improve programs and services, manage resources wisely, and increase retention rates for students. These data must also be used to document students' successes, specifically, not just the traditional measures of success such as graduation or transfer, but also job attainment, increase in job level, completion of a certificate, or even a smaller measure such as completion of a course or series of courses (such as remediation) that take students to the next step of their academic career.

Other public policy issues surface periodically with the passage of federal legislation that affects community colleges, including the Carl D. Perkins Vocational and Applied Technology Act, the Workforce Investment Act, and the Higher Education Act. Recent legislative proposals have focused on the enrollment of undocumented immigrants and international students in American colleges and universities.

These laws and similar legislative initiatives will continue to affect funding and thus dictate the college's ability to educate workers, provide financial aid, and reduce barriers to enrollment. Community college leaders will have to take an active role at both the state and federal levels as the public policies embodied in such legislation is formulated.

In the face of the challenges that lie ahead—surging enrollments, new student demographics, new teaching and learning approaches, continued emphasis on preparing a world-class workforce, cycles of economic growth and recession, and globalization—community colleges will undoubtedly choose the path of innovation. The new generation of presidents that is now assuming leadership will bring new skills and talents to bear as they guide their colleges into the future. Having achieved organizational maturity, community colleges may well evolve into something different, but they will still remain true to their core values of access, academic excellence, and student-centeredness. ⊕

Figure 6.1

U.S. Population Projection: 2000–2050

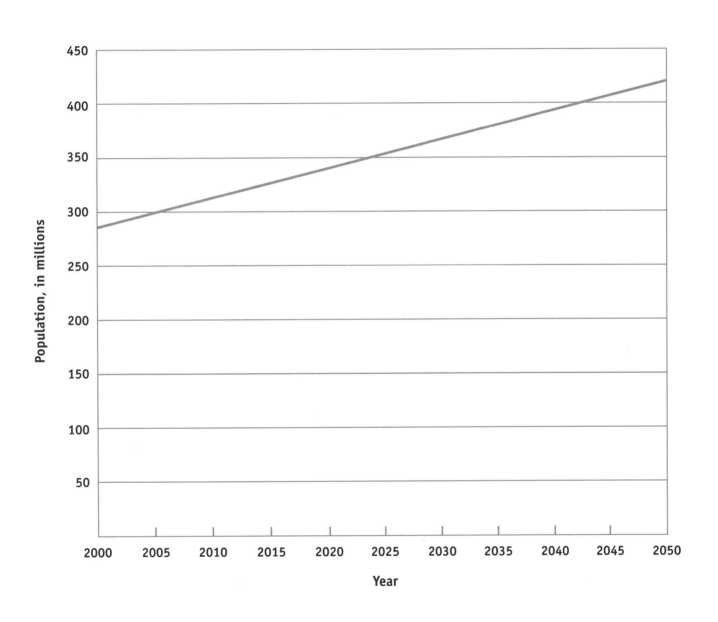

Source: U.S. Census Bureau (2004c)

Figure 6.2

Projected Percentage of White Non-Hispanics and Minorities in the U.S. Population: 2000–2050

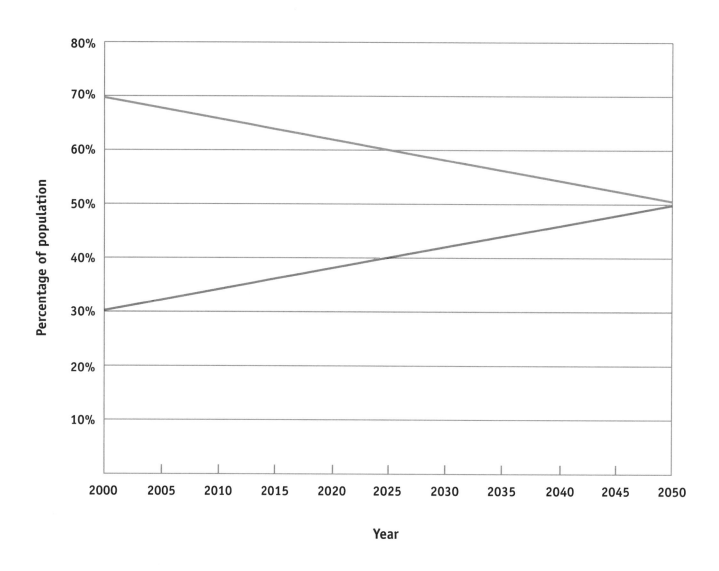

Source: U.S. Census Bureau (2004c)

Figure 6.3

Number of High School Graduates, Actual and Projected: 1988–2013

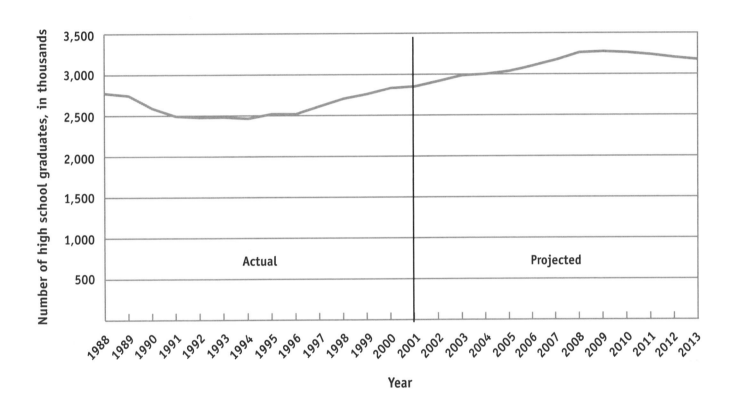

Source: Herald & Hussar (2004)

Figure 6.4

Associate Degrees Awarded, Actual and Projected: 1988–2013

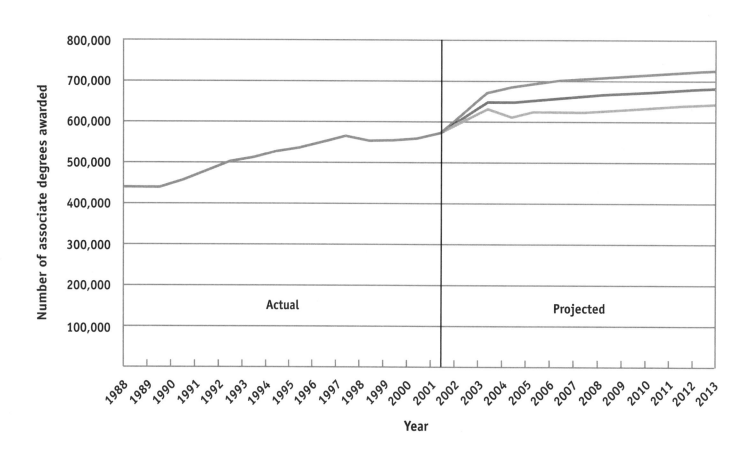

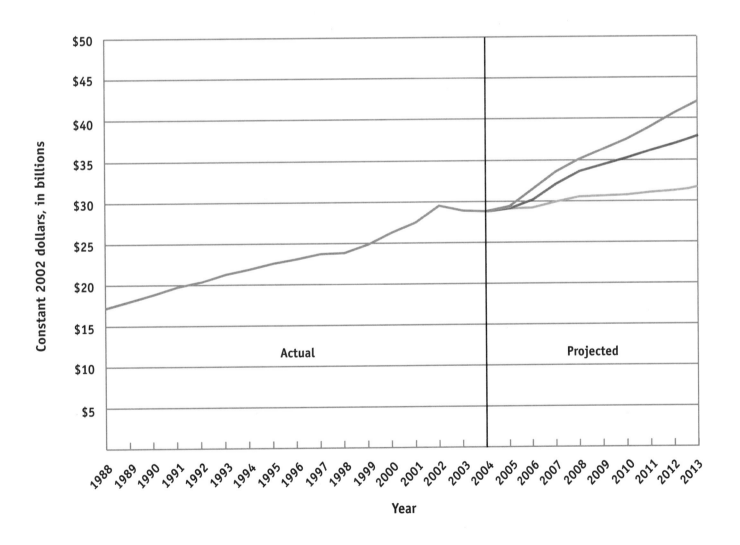

Figure 6.5

Public Community College Educational and General Expenditures, Actual and Projected: 1988–2013

Projected
— High
— Middle
— Low

Constant 2002 dollars, in billions

Actual

Projected

Year

Source: Herald & Hussar (2004)

Figure 6.6

Enrollment at Public Community Colleges, Actual and Projected: 1988–2013

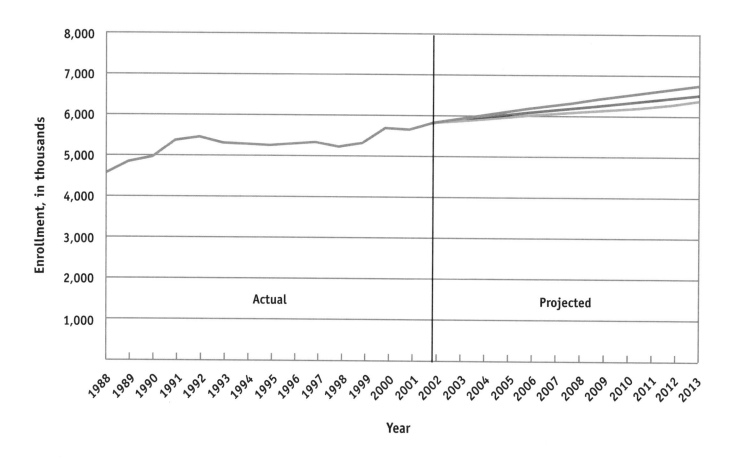

Source: Herald & Hussar (2004)

Figure 6.7
Enrollment at Independent Community Colleges, Actual and Projected: 1988–2013

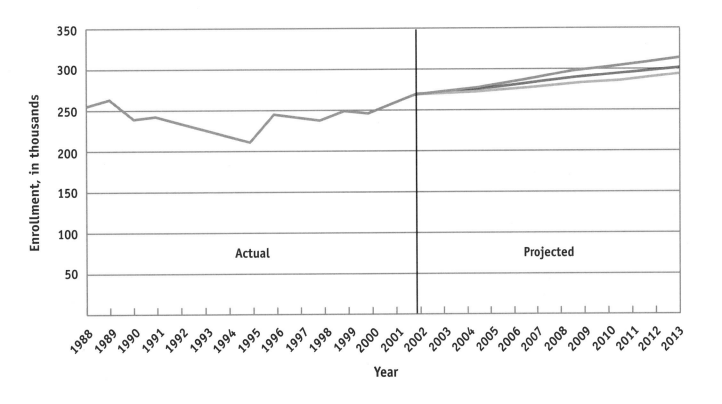

Source: Herald & Hussar (2004)

Figure 6.8

Full-Time Equivalent College Enrollment, Actual and Projected: 1988–2013

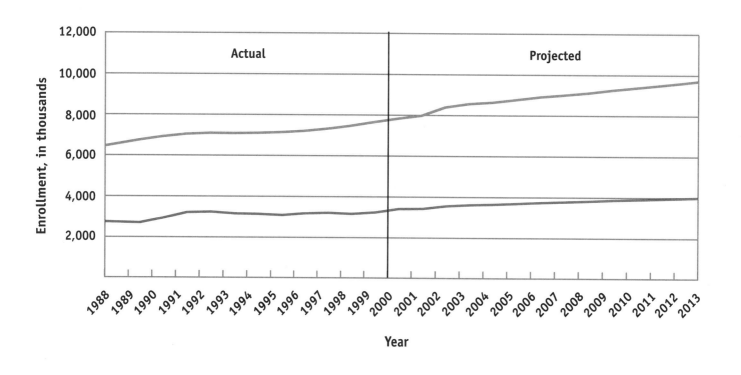

Source: Herald & Hussar (2004)

TABLE 6.1

**Occupations With the Largest Projected Job Growth:
2002–2012 (numbers in thousands)**

Occupation	# of Employees		Change, 2002–2012	
	2002	2012	#	%
Registered nurses	2,284	2,908	623	27%
Postsecondary teachers	1,581	2,184	603	38%
Retail salespersons	4,076	4,672	596	15%
Customer service representatives	1,894	2,354	460	24%
Food prep and food services workers	1,990	2,444	454	23%
Cashiers, except gaming	3,432	3,886	454	13%
Janitors and cleaners	2,267	2,681	414	18%
General and operations managers	2,049	2,425	376	18%
Waiters and waitresses	2,097	2,464	367	18%
Nursing aides	1,375	1,718	343	25%

Source: Hecker (2004)

TABLE 6.2

**Occupations With the Fastest Projected Job Growth:
2002–2012 (numbers in thousands)**

Occupation	# of Employees		Change, 2002–2012	
	2002	2012	#	%
Medical assistants	365	579	215	59%
Network system and data communications analysts	186	292	106	57%
Physician assistants	63	94	31	49%
Social and human service assistants	305	454	149	49%
Home health aides	580	859	279	48%
Medical records and health information technicians	147	216	69	47%
Physical therapist aides	37	54	17	46%
Computer software engineers, applications	394	573	179	46%
Computer software engineers, system software	281	409	128	45%
Physical therapist assistants	50	73	22	45%

Source: Hecker (2004)

TABLE 6.3
Occupations With the Largest Projected Job Declines: 2002–2012 (numbers in thousands)

Occupation	# of Employees		Change, 2002–2012	
	2002	2012	#	%
Farmers and ranchers	1,158	920	-238	-21%
Sewing machine operators	315	216	-99	-31%
Word processors and typists	241	148	-93	-39%
Stock clerks and order fillers	1,628	1,560	-68	-4%
Secretaries, except legal, medical, executive	1,975	1,918	-57	-3%
Electrical and electronic equipment assemblers	281	230	-51	-18%
Computer operators	182	151	-30	-17%
Telephone operators	50	22	-28	-56%
Postal service mail sorters and processors	253	226	-26	-10%
Loan interviewers and clerks	170	146	-24	-14%

Source: Hecker (2004)

GLOSSARY

academic support: expenditures for support services that are an integral part of the institution's primary mission of instruction, research, or public service.

associate degree: an award that normally requires at least 2 but fewer than 4 years of full-time-equivalent college work.

attainment: the highest level of education a student completed.

Baccalaureate and Beyond Study (B&B): longitudinal studies that follow first-time baccalaureate recipients for 5 years or more. Recipients are a subsample of the students in the National Postsecondary Student Aid Study.

Beginning Postsecondary Student Study (BPS): a longitudinal study that follows first-time freshmen for 5 years or more. These students are a subsample of the students in the National Postsecondary Student Aid Study.

branch campus: an affiliated campus of a college that is not separately accredited and does not separately offer a degree.

campus-based aid: student financial aid from federal, state, and local governments administered through the institution, not directly to the student. An example is College Work-Study.

certificate: a formal award certifying the satisfactory completion of a postsecondary program.

College Work-Study: a program in which a student is paid through federal and matching institutional funds for work on the campus or on its behalf.

community college (AACC definition): an institution that is accredited (or undergoing accreditation) by one of the six regional accrediting bodies and primarily offers the associate degree as the highest degree. A community college can also be a campus that offers the associate degree as the highest award but is part of a regionally accredited, baccalaureate-granting institution.

community college (U.S. Department of Education definition): an institution of higher education that is accredited by an agency recognized by the Department of Education and offers the associate degree as the highest award.

constant dollars: the value of the dollar adjusted for the impact of inflation. The Consumer Price Index was used to adjust for the effects of inflation.

current dollars: the actual dollar value, not adjusted for inflation.

Current Population Survey (CPS): a monthly survey of about 50,000 households conducted by the U.S. Census Bureau for the Bureau of Labor Statistics. Respondents are interviewed to obtain information about the employment status of each member of the household aged 15 or older.

degree-seeking students: students enrolled in courses for credit who are recognized by the institution as seeking a degree or formal award.

employment status (faculty and staff): full-time or part-time status as determined by the institution.

fall headcount enrollment: the number of students enrolled in courses creditable toward a diploma, certificate, degree, or other formal award, as of October 15 (or the institution's official fall reporting date). Includes students who are part of vocational or occupational programs and students enrolled in off-campus centers.

federal aid: any financial aid provided to students by the federal government.

federal revenue: includes both restricted and unrestricted appropriations, grants, gifts, and contracts from federal sources, except for Pell Grant dollars, which are separately reported, unless otherwise noted.

field of study: the primary field of study a degree or certificate was awarded in, as classified by the institution based on guidelines developed by the U.S. Department of Education.

financial aid: any of a wide variety of programs designed to aid a student financially to attend a postsecondary institution.

first-generation student: student whose parents have had no postsecondary education.

first-time, first-year student: a student attending any institution for the first time at the undergraduate level.

four-year college: a college that offers a baccalaureate or higher degree as its primary award.

full-time employment: 35 or more hours per week.

full-time student: a student enrolled for 12 or more credits (24 or more contact hours a week).

full-year unduplicated headcount: the number of students enrolled during the 12-month reporting period in any courses leading to a degree or other formal award, and the number of students enrolled in courses that are part of a terminal vocational or occupational program.

independent (private) college: a college operated by privately appointed officials, which derives its funding primarily from private sources.

independent student: according to federal financial aid guidelines, students are considered independent if they meet any of the following criteria: age 24 or older, veteran of the U.S. armed forces, enrolled in a graduate or professional program (beyond a bachelor's degree), married, orphan or ward of the court, or have legal dependents other than a spouse. In addition, financial aid officers may designate students who do not meet these criteria to be independent if the students can document they are in fact self-supporting.

institutional aid: any aid the college provides to the student to help defray the cost of attending the college.

institutional support: expenditures for day-to-day operations established to provide service and maintenance of grounds and facilities used for educational and general purposes.

instruction: category of expenditures that includes all expenditures for instruction and instructors' salaries, including both credit and noncredit academic instruction.

Integrated Postsecondary Educational Data System (IPEDS): a series of surveys conducted by the U.S. Department of Education. The surveys provide aggregate data at the college level and cover topics such as enrollment, institutional finances, institutional characteristics, degree and certificate completion, staff and faculty status, faculty salaries, and, soon, student graduation and transfer activities.

international programs: programs that deal with training students in countries other than the United States or programs that specialize in teaching about other countries.

local revenue: category of revenue that includes both restricted and unrestricted appropriations, grants, gifts, and local sources, unless otherwise noted.

National Postsecondary Student Aid Study (NPSAS): a survey conducted by the U.S. Department of Education every three or four years. Data is collected on a stratified random sample of students from all levels of postsecondary institutions eligible for student financial aid; the best source for nationally representative data on financial aid, student finances, and other individual student characteristics.

National Study of Postsecondary Faculty (NSOPF): a survey conducted every six or so years by the U.S. Department of Education. Data is collected on a stratified random sample of instructional faculty from all levels of postsecondary institutions. NSOPF is one of the best sources of information available about faculty at community colleges.

part-time employment: fewer than 35 hours per week.

part-time student: a student enrolled for 11 or fewer credits (fewer than 24 contact hours a week).

Pell Grant: federally funded grants to students based on family financial need; includes all federal Pell Grant funds received by the college.

per capita (state): total amount of funds divided by the total population of the state.

persistence: whether a student is still pursuing a degree or certificate by attending a postsecondary institution.

private gifts, grants, and contracts: revenues from private donors, private contracts, and foreign governments.

proprietary college: a for-profit college run by private citizens or corporations.

public college: a college that is operated by publicly elected or appointed officials and that derives its funding primarily from public sources.

public service: category of funds budgeted to provide noninstructional services beneficial to groups external to the institution.

race/ethnicity: racial or ethnic category that people identify with, according to the terminology used by the U.S. Department of Education: Black, non-Hispanic; American Indian or Alaskan native; Asian or Pacific Islander; Hispanic; White, non-Hispanic.

remedial education: courses in reading, writing, or mathematics for college students lacking the skills necessary to perform work at the level required by the institution.

replacement value: estimated cost to replace buildings and equipment owned, rented, or used by the institution.

research: funds spent to produce research outcomes commissioned by an agency either external to the institution or separately budgeted by an organizational unit within the institution.

service learning: a program integrated into curriculum in which a student volunteers as part of his or her coursework and integrates this service activity into the learning experience.

state aid: any student financial aid provided by a state government.

state revenue: category of revenue that includes both restricted and unrestricted appropriations, grants, gifts, and contracts from state sources, unless otherwise noted.

student services: expenditures for admissions, registration, and activities whose primary purpose is to contribute to students' emotional and physical well-being and to their intellectual, cultural, and social development outside the context of the formal instructional program.

subsidized loans: loans to students to help defray attendance costs, where interest accrual is paid for while the student is still pursuing a degree. Includes Perkins loans and some Stafford loans.

Title IV institution: an institution that meets the federal guidelines to receive federal funds as a part of Title IV of the Higher Education Act.

transfer: academic transition in which a student stops attending one college to begin attending another, often with credits earned at the first institution transferring to apply for credit at the second institution.

tribal college: a college operated by a Native American nation.

tuition and fees: the average annual amount a student spends to attend classes full time. Tuition and fees do not include books and supplies, room and board, or living expenses.

unsubsidized loans: loans to students to help defray attendance costs, where interest accrues to the student's loan amount while he or she is still pursuing a degree. Unsubsidized loans include PLUS, SLA, and some Stafford loans.

workforce training: education programs designed to increase skills needed for specific jobs.

REFERENCES

American Association of Community Colleges. (2004a). *2004 demographics: Community college presidents* [Electronic fact sheet]. Retrieved June 1, 2004, from http://www.ccleadership.org/resource_center/demo_snapshots.htm

American Association of Community Colleges. (2004b). AACC membership database [Data file]. Washington, DC: American Association of Community Colleges.

American Association of Community Colleges & Association of Community College Trustees. (2000). *The knowledge net: Connecting communities, learners, and colleges.* Washington, DC: Community College Press.

American Association of University Professors. (2004). *Don't blame faculty for high tuition: The annual report on the economic status of the profession, 2003–2004.* Washington, DC: Author.

Association of Community College Trustees. (2003, September 18). *Community colleges put more dollars than they cost in public pockets* [Press release]. Retrieved March 8, 2004, from http://acct.org/about/Press/091803press.htm

Berger, L. (2002, August 4). The rise of the perma-temp [Education Life section]. *The New York Times,* pp. 20–23.

Blair, D., Phinney, L., & Phillippe, K. A. (2001). *International programs at community colleges* [Research brief]. Washington, DC: American Association of Community Colleges.

Blount, P., & Associates, Inc., & Lindley, A. (2005). *Compensation and benefits of community college CEOs: 2004* [Research brief]. Washington, DC: American Association of Community Colleges.

Choy, S. P. (2004). *Paying for college: Changes between 1990 and 2000 for full-time dependent undergraduates* (NCES 2004–075). Washington, DC: U.S. Department of Education, National Center for Education Statistics.

Cohen, A. M., & Brawer, F. B. (2003). *The American community college* (4th ed.). San Francisco: Jossey-Bass.

College Board. (2004). *Trends in student aid: 2004.* Washington, DC: Author.

Community College Survey of Student Engagement. (2002). *Engaging community colleges: A first look.* Austin, TX: Author.

Community College Survey of Student Engagement. (2003). *Engaging community colleges: National benchmarks of quality.* Austin, TX: Author.

Education Commission of the States. (2000). *State funding for community colleges: A 50-state survey.* Denver: Author.

Education Commission of the States. (2003). *Closing the college participation gap.* Denver: Author.

Evelyn, J. (2004, April 30). Community colleges at a crossroads. *The Chronicle of Higher Education,* pp. A27–28.

Hecker, D. E. (2004). Employment outlook: 2002–12: Occupational employment projections to 2012. *Monthly Labor Review, 127*(2), 80–105.

Herald, D. G., & Hussar, W. J. (2004). *Projections of education statistics to 2013* (NCES 2004-013). Washington, DC: U.S. Department of Education, National Center for Education Statistics.

Hoachlander, G., Sikora, A. C., & Horn, L. (2003). *Community college students: Goals, academic preparation, and outcomes* (NCES 2003–164). Washington, DC: U.S. Department of Education, National Center for Education Statistics.

Horn, L. J. (1996). *Nontraditional undergraduates: Trends in enrollment from 1986 to 1992 and persistence and attainment among 1989–90 beginning postsecondary students* (NCES 97-578). U.S. Department of Education, National Center for Education Statistics. Washington, DC: U.S. Government Printing Office.

Illinois Community College Board. (2002). *Fact sheet: Economic impact Illinois' 39 community college districts* [Research report]. Springfield, IL: Author.

Knapp, L. G., Kelly, J. E., Whitmore, R. W., Wu, S., Levine, B., Huh, S., & Broyles, S. (2004). *Enrollment in postsecondary institutions: Fall 2001 and financial statistics, fiscal year 2001* (NCES 2004-155). Washington, DC: U.S. Department of Education, National Center for Education Statistics.

Lane, K. (2003, February 17). How much is too much: What happens when the least expensive college education becomes too expensive? *Community College Week*, pp. 7–9.

Los Angeles Community Colleges. (2002). *The economic impact of the Los Angeles Community Colleges* [Research report]. Retrieved March 8, 2004 from http://research.laccd.edu/research/General/Ecimpact.htm

McPhee, S. (2004). *Hot programs at community colleges* [Research brief]. Washington, DC: American Association of Community Colleges.

Merisotis, J. P., & Wolanin, T. R. (2000). *Community college financing: Strategies and challenges* (New Expeditions Issues Paper No. 5). Washington, DC: American Association of Community Colleges.

Mortenson, T. G. (2000). Poverty, race, and the failure of public policy: The crisis of access in higher education. *Academe, 6,* 38–40.

National Center for Education Statistics. (1996). 1995–1996 national postsecondary student aid study. Washington, DC: U.S. Department of Education.

National Center for Education Statistics. (2004a). *Baccalaureate and beyond longitudinal study: First follow-up (B&B:99/01)* Washington, DC: U.S.

Department of Education. Available from the Data Analysis System Web site, http://www.nces.ed.gov/das

National Center for Education Statistics. (2004b). *Beginning postsecondary students longitudinal study: Second follow-up (BPS:96/01)* (NCES 2003-163). Washington, DC: U.S. Department of Education. Available from the Data Analysis System Web site, http://www.nces.ed.gov/das

National Center for Education Statistics. (2004c). *Integrated postsecondary education data system (IPEDS) completions survey* [Data file]. Washington, DC: U.S. Department of Education.

National Center for Education Statistics. (2004d). *Integrated postsecondary education data system (IPEDS) employees by assigned position survey* [Data file]. Washington, DC: U.S. Department of Education.

National Center for Education Statistics. (2004e). *Integrated postsecondary education data system (IPEDS) fall enrollment survey* [Data file]. Washington, DC: U.S. Department of Education.

National Center for Education Statistics. (2004f). *Integrated postsecondary education data system (IPEDS) fall staff survey* [Data file]. Washington, DC: U.S. Department of Education.

National Center for Education Statistics. (2004g). *Integrated postsecondary education data system (IPEDS) finance survey* [Data file]. Washington, DC: U.S. Department of Education.

National Center for Education Statistics. (2004h). *Integrated postsecondary education data system (IPEDS) institutional characteristics survey* [Data file]. Washington, DC: U.S. Department of Education.

National Center for Education Statistics. (2004i). *National postsecondary student aid study: 1995–96.* Washington, DC: U.S. Department of Education. Available from the Data Analysis System Web site, http://www.nces.ed.gov/das

National Center for Education Statistics. (2004j).

National postsecondary student aid study: 1999–2000. Washington, DC: U.S. Department of Education. Available from the Data Analysis System Web site, http://www.nces.ed.gov/das

National Center for Education Statistics. (2004k). *National study of postsecondary faculty:1998–99.* Washington, DC: U.S. Department of Education. Available from the Data Analysis System Web site, http://www.nces.ed.gov/das

National Center for Education Statistics. (2005). *National postsecondary student aid study: 2003–2004.* Washington, DC: U.S. Department of Education. Available from the Data Analysis System Web site, http://www.nces.ed.gov/das

National Council for State Boards of Nursing. (2004a). NCLEX statistics from NCSBN: 2000. Chicago, IL: Author.

National Council for State Boards of Nursing. (2004b). NCLEX statistics from NCSBN: 2001. Chicago, IL: Author.

National Council for State Boards of Nursing. (2004c). NCLEX statistics from NCSBN: 2002. Chicago, IL: Author.

National Council for State Boards of Nursing. (2004d). NCLEX statistics from NCSBN: 2003. Chicago, IL: Author.

National Council for State Boards of Nursing. (2004e). NCLEX statistics from NCSBN: 2004. Chicago, IL: Author.

Nock, M. M., & Shults, C. (2001). *Hot programs at community colleges* [Research brief]. Washington, DC: Community College Press.

O'Banion, T. (1997). *A learning college for the 21st century.* Washington, DC: ACE/Oryx Press.

Phillippe, K., & Eblinger, I. R. (1998). *Community college foundations: Funding the community college future.* Washington, DC: American Association of Community Colleges.

Prentice, M., Robinson, G., & McPhee, S. (2003). *Service learning in community colleges: 2003 national survey results* [Research brief]. Washington, DC: American Association of Community Colleges.

Selingo, J. (2003, May 2). What Americans think about higher education. *The Chronicle of Higher Education,* pp. A11–A16.

Selingo, J. (2004, May 7). U.S. public's confidence in colleges remains high. *The Chronicle of Higher Education,* p. A35.

Shults, C. (2001). *The critical impact of impending retirements on community college leadership* [Research brief]. Washington, DC: American Association of Community Colleges.

Snyder, T. D. (1999). *Digest of education statistics: 1998* (NCES 2001-034). Washington, DC: U.S. Department of Education, National Center for Education Statistics.

Snyder, T. D. (2003). *Digest of education statistics: 2002* (NCES 2003–060). Washington, DC: U.S. Department of Education, National Center for Education Statistics.

Snyder, T. D., & Hoffman, C. M. (2001). *Digest of education statistics: 2000* (NCES 2001-034). Washington, DC: U.S. Department of Education, National Center for Education Statistics.

U.S. Census Bureau. (1998). *State population estimates: Annual time series, July 1, 1990 to July 1, 1997.* Washington, DC: U.S. Department of Commerce.

U.S. Census Bureau. (1999). *Educational attainment in the United States: March 1998.* Washington, DC: U.S. Department of Commerce.

U.S. Census Bureau. (2000). *Educational attainment in the United States: March 1999.* Washington, DC: U.S. Department of Commerce.

U.S. Census Bureau. (2001). *Educational attainment in the United States: March 2000.* Washington, DC: U.S. Department of Commerce.

U.S. Census Bureau. (2002). *The big payoff: Educational attainment and synthetic estimates of work-life earnings*. Washington, DC: U.S. Department of Commerce.

U.S. Census Bureau. (2004a). *Educational attainment in the United States: March 2001 and March 2002*. Washington, DC: U.S. Department of Commerce.

U.S. Census Bureau. (2004b). *State population estimates: Annual estimates of the population by sex and age: April 1, 2000 to July 1, 2003 (SC-EST2003-02-01)*. Washington, DC: U.S. Department of Commerce.

U.S. Census Bureau. (2004c). *U.S. interim projections by age, sex, race, and Hispanic origin*. Washington, DC: U.S. Department of Commerce.

VanDerLinden, K. E. (2002). *Credit student analysis: 1999 and 2000* (Faces of the Future). Washington, DC: American Association of Community Colleges.

Virginia Community College System. (2003, April 9). Study shows community colleges make major impact on commonwealth's economy [Press release]. Retrieved March 8, 2004 from http://www.vccs.edu/aboutvccs/news_releases/economicimpact.htm

Waits, T., & Lewis, L. (2003). *Distance education at degree-granting postsecondary institutions: 2000–2001* (NCES 2003-017). Washington, DC: U.S. Department of Education, National Center for Education Statistics.

Wei, C. C., Li, X., & Berkner, L. (2004). *A decade of undergraduate student aid: 1989–90 to 1999–2000* (NCES 2004-158). Washington, DC: U.S. Department of Education, National Center for Education Statistics. Wellman, J. V. (2002). *State policy and community college baccalaureate transfer*. Washington, DC: National Center for Public Policy and Higher Education.

INDEX

ABOUT THE AUTHORS

Kent A. Phillippe, a senior research associate, has been instrumental in developing a strong, reliable research capacity at the American Association of Community Colleges (AACC) for 10 years. He has integrated diverse national data sets from sources including the U.S. Census Bureau, the U.S. Department of Education, and AACC data files to better understand and describe community colleges and the communities they serve. These integrations have been integral in producing publications widely used as resources for information on community colleges and in providing a rich resource for survey research and project-specific college selections based on predefined criteria. Phillippe serves on advisory panels for national research projects including the U.S. Department of Education's National Postsecondary Student Aid Study, the Beginning Postsecondary Student Longitudinal Study, and the National Study of Postsecondary Faculty, as well as projects funded by the U.S. Department of Labor, the Lumina Foundation, and the Fund for the Improvement of Postsecondary Education. Phillippe has a BA in psychology from Hamline University and an MA in clinical and counseling psychology from Southern Methodist University; he attended a Michigan State University doctoral program in child/family clinical psychology.

Leila González Sullivan is the W. Dallas Herring Professor of Community College Education in the Department of Adult and Community College Education (ACCE) at North Carolina State University, where she teaches graduate courses and serves as executive director of the National Initiative for Institutional Effectiveness. She also directs the Hispanic Leadership Fellows Program for the National Community College Hispanic Council (NCCHC) and the Department Chairs Institute sponsored by the ACCE department. Prior to this appointment, Sullivan was the interim director of community college relations at The College Board in New York. She was president of the Community College of Baltimore County, Essex Campus (1996–1999), after serving as president of Middlesex Community College (CT) and interim president of Gateway Community College (CT). Sullivan has been involved in the community college movement at the national, regional, and local levels for many years. She was a member of the board of directors of the American Association for Community Colleges (1993–1996 and 1999–2002). She was national president of the American Association for Women in Community Colleges (AAWCC) and is currently legislative liaison for its board (in 1998, she received AAWCC's Carolyn Desjardins President of the Year award). She has served on the AACC Commission on Learning and Communications Technologies and served as secretary and vice president of the NCCHC board (1991–2000). Sullivan holds an EdD degree in vocational education administration and an EdS in adult education, both from the University of Arkansas. She earned an MA in Spanish literature from New York University and a baccalaureate in English literature from Trinity College in Washington, DC. In May 1997, she received the Trinity College Centennial Alumnae Award for Academic Excellence.